S A N F O R D   P I N S K E R

THE COMEDY THAT "HOITS"

A N   E S S A Y   O N   T H E   F I C T I O N   O F
P H I L I P   R O T H

A   L I T E R A R Y   F R O N T I E R S   E D I T I O N
U N I V E R S I T Y   O F   M I S S O U R I   P R E S S
C O L U M B I A

Acknowledgments

I would like to express my sincere thanks to those who have been especially helpful in this project: to students at Franklin and Marshall College who looked skeptical and made me try again; to Peter Young and Robert Siever who helped more than the Fackenthal Library should ever know; to Thomas Lloyd who gave sound editorial advice and much encouragement; and, finally, to my wife Ann who would have spent a semester in Newark, New Jersey, if necessary.

Goodbye Columbus. by Philip Roth. Copyright © 1959 by Philip Roth. Excerpts reprinted by permission of the publisher Houghton Mifflin Company.

Acknowledgment is extended to Random House, Inc., for permission to quote from the following copyrighted works of Philip Roth: *Letting Go, When She Was Good, Portnoy's Complaint,* and *Our Gang.*

Excerpt material from *The Breast* by Philip Roth. Copyright © 1972 by Philip Roth. Reprinted by permission of Holt, Rinehart and Winston, Publishers. From *The Great American Novel* by Philip Roth. Copyright © 1973 by Philip Roth. Reprinted by permission of Holt, Rinehart and Winston, Publishers. From *My Life as a Man* by Philip Roth. Copyright © 1970, 1971, 1973, 1974 by Philip Roth. Reprinted by permission of Holt, Rinehart and Winston, Publishers.

ISBN 0–8262–0181–4
Copyright © 1975 by
The Curators of the University of Missouri
Library of Congress Catalog Card Number 75–16210
Printed and bound in the United States of America
University of Missouri Press, Columbia, Missouri 65201

Library of Congress Cataloging in Publication Data
Pinsker, Sanford.
   The comedy that "hoits."
   (A Literary frontiers edition)
   1. Roth, Philip—Criticism and interpretation—
Addresses, essays, lectures.   I.   Title.
PS3568.O855Z84   813'.5'4   75–16210
ISBN 0–8262–0181–4

For my Mother, who hoped I would write about somebody else.

THE COMEDY THAT "HOITS"

F*innegans Wake* may be responsible for our fascination with endings that circle back, ineluctably, to beginnings, with symmetries more often critically imagined than real. After all, not every canon is Joycean, nor every author Joyce. But an innocence about books, once lost, is hard to recapture; we have learned to sniff out correspondences and to savor their various aromas. Philip Roth's latest novel, *My Life as a Man*, teases us into thoughts of an *oeuvre* that begins with the testy Neil Klugman of "Goodbye, Columbus" and ends with the autobiographical "confessions" of Peter Tarnopol. Newark figures as a prominent backdrop for both protagonists, the Hudson (rather than the Liffey) riverrunning past Roth's Eves and Adams.

That Roth was born in the same New Jersey town that produced the likes of Leslie Fiedler, Allen Ginsberg, and LeRoi Jones confirms our suspicions about future authors having the good luck and better timing to be where the "hot center" is going to happen. To be sure, Fiedler has long since "lit out"—like his prototype, Huck Finn—for that mythic West where the dreams of black men merge with those of Indians, and all men, at bottom, turn out to be Fiedleresque Jews. Ginsberg has become an international citizen on behalf of counterculture theatricality, and Jones has metamorphosed into Imamu Amiri Baraka, more a native son of Africa than Newark. Only Roth seems inextricably tied to the apron strings of his birthplace across the river from New York and the seriocomic American-Jewish upbringing he received there.

Philip Roth's career, for all its brevity, affirms certain axiomatic truths about contemporary American fiction: (1) that the purely personal can, with insistence, become the publicly important; (2) that nothing quite succeeds like an interesting "failure"; (3) that satire carries as many unearned assets as it does undeserved liabilities. I might express it another way: The truth about the value of Philip Roth's work lies somewhere between the lavish praise and the lingering sense of disappointment it has generated; he is a writer of brilliant talents, all too often brilliantly wasted. His novels, taken as a whole, leave one with the uneasy feeling that he has not yet been tested by a subject big enough to demand as much from his heart as we have come to expect from his mouth.

If Norman Podhoretz is correct, Roth has a simple enough point to make—that "Americans are disgusting people."[1] And, yet, Podhoretz's assessment, however shrewd, hardly settles the nagging questions raised in one insistent novel after another. After all, the same reduction might be applied to a great many serious American writers with whom Roth is seldom compared and never confused: Hawthorne, Melville, Twain. Besides, a writer's "point," even one he endlessly seems bent upon proving, may be less important than the fiction generated in the process. Whatever flames of controversy were kindled by *Goodbye, Columbus* have burned even more brightly in the seven books that followed. At a time when the very "fictionality" of fiction is called into serious question, when invitations to attend the burial of "conventional" novels are extended regularly and *reportage* threatens to replace imaginative dreaming with brutal "facts," Philip Roth remains a fresh burst of air indeed. More-

1. Norman Podhoretz, "Laureate of the New Class," *Commentary*, LIV: 6 (December 1972), 4.

over, serious writers are always the bearers of bad news to readers who would prefer hearing that they are the "fairest of them all." That "Americans are disgusting people" may well have been *what* Roth has been saying, but it is the *how* and *why* of it that merits our attention.

Finally, a word or two about the title of this book: I have chosen "The Comedy That 'Hoits'" to suggest a correspondence between the public dimensions of Roth's scathing satire and the private realm of his self-abasement. Like D. H. Lawrence, Philip Roth is a writer out to "shed his sickness" in the discipline and pattern-making of art. But if Nottingham has provided the socioeconomic conditions from which "tragedy" could be fashioned, locating any situation in Newark threatens to drown emotions into the vulgarity of an American-Jewish joke. As its pathetic victim and/or sarcastic victimizer, Alexander Portnoy puts it this way: "Spring me from this role I play of the smothered son in the Jewish joke! Because it's beginning to pall a little, at thirty-three! And also it *hoits*, you know, there is *pain* involved, a little human suffering is being felt. . . ."

Discovering a technique to not only deal with *hoit* but to transcend its crippling power has been the central concern of Roth's fiction. The pains joyfully confessed—as well as those artfully concealed—tell us much about Roth and even more about the nature of contemporary fiction. It is a story that begins with that exercise in moral earnestness we have learned to call "Goodbye, Columbus."

NEWARK, THROUGH A
GLASS DARKLY

G*oodbye, Columbus and Five Short Stories* was
published in 1959, at a moment conveniently wedged
between the innocence that had characterized the 1950s
and the permissiveness that was to dominate the next
decade. For better or worse Philip Roth became a remarkably accurate barometer of the radical shift occur-
ring in our national sensibility. To be sure, the benefit
of hindsight turns such judgments into easy com-
monplaces; in 1959 *Goodbye, Columbus* looked very
odd indeed. On one hand, it was F. Scott Fitzgerald's
This Side of Paradise in an American-Jewish idiom; on
the other, it was satire à la Evelyn Waugh, but without
the saving graces of his urbane civility. In *Goodbye,
Columbus*, Roth demonstrated that he had the potential
of many young artists. After all, we are no longer sur-
prised when a young author makes his debut in a hard-
cover collection of short stories, filled with serious (i.e.
"sensitive") young protagonists, thinly veiled autobiographical conflicts, and ample evidence that the budding artist has been a careful worker. Such books are
dutifully praised and, just as dutifully, forgotten, but
Roth added some touches not included in the standard
scenario. The work not only won its twenty-six-year-
old author a National Book Award, but, more importantly, it changed the very ground rules by which one
wrote about American-Jewish life. As the critical con-
census would have it now: If an older generation of
American-Jewish writers had insisted, in Bernard
Malamud's phrase, that "All men are Jews!" Roth's
vision was the converse—all Jews were also men.

Granted, he was not the first American-Jewish writer to cross verbal swords with the official Jewish community. Artists, regardless of ethnic affiliation, rarely cultivate good public relations. As early as 1917 charges about "self-hatred" and "Jewish anti-Semitism" had been leveled against Abraham Cahan, the author of an unflattering study called *The Rise of David Levinsky*. Secular writing—whether in the newly acquired English of Cahan or the Yiddish of a satirist like Mendele—was followed by the predictable slings and arrows of outraged rabbis. But Roth's book brought the longstanding antagonisms to a rapid boil. To be sure, no social critic has an easy lot. The "glad tidings" they bring about us are never welcome and, quite understandably, offended readers go to great lengths to prove that such writers are (a) morbidly misanthropic, (b) clearly immoral, (c) merely insane—or, as in Roth's case, all of the above. Defenses concerning the purely literary nature of American-Jewish fiction never answer the feckless attacks by well-meaning rabbis nor do the floating objections ever really stop.

In other words, *Goodbye, Columbus* was born in a swirl of controversy, and the recent film version simply gave a second wind to those who may have missed the book when it first appeared. I am also suggesting (somewhat more timidly) that the novella itself tends to get lost in the shuffle of allegiances. Nearly half the pages of *Goodbye, Columbus* are devoted to the title story, an oppressively earnest look at the ill-fated love affair between Neil Klugman and Brenda Patimkin. And, yet, for all the uncompromising "toughness" about love, its real concerns are socioeconomic rather than erotic.

"Goodbye, Columbus" begins, as it must, at the

poolside. For at least a full generation American Jews have been replacing the squalor of Lower East Side tenements with the affluence of suburban ranchers, the ritual bath with kidney-shaped swimming pools. Warnings about the ashy taste "success" is likely to have had been sounded before—in *The Rise of David Levinsky* and, later, in the socialist spirit of proletarian fiction. But Roth's devastating, albeit realistic, eye for the undercutting detail is disturbing in ways that even the most dedicated ideologue could not achieve. This particular mirror held up to American-Jewish nature "hurt." Moreover, it was meant to.

Neil Klugman's alternating currents of attraction-and-repulsion for the ethos that produces a Brenda Patimkin are foreshadowed in the opening scene. Brenda casually asks Neil to hold her glasses and dives, myopically, into the country club pool. Effectively reduced to the status of impromptu servant, Neil is nonetheless fascinated by "her head of short-clipped auburn hair held up, straight ahead of her, as though it were a rose on a long stem," her svelte, athletic body and the easy way in which her hand extends to retrieve the glasses he has been breathlessly holding. Brenda is one born to the Jewish-American princesshood, and her manner reflects the treatment she unconsciously expects.

What Brenda will later come to call Neil's "nastiness" has to do with his awkward role as an initiate into the mysteries of Short Hills life. "Goodbye, Columbus" is, in effect, the Cinderella story turned upside down until the poor kid plays Prince Charming and the skullery maiden enters the stage with glass slippers already on. Neil lugs his ambivalent thoughts about Newark into a wasteland of conspicuous consumption (endless eating) and nonstop leisure. In terms

6

of class conflict, it is the "have-nots" of Newark against the "haves" of Short Hills, although Roth seems less sure about such rigid categorizations than did writers in the thirties. Neil wants an independence from both factions, one as pristine in its innocence as it is radical in implication. Presumably this lack of vested interests provides the edge that a satiric persona requires: Neil can (presumably) judge each world from the vantage point of semiobjective distance.

But it is hard to see exactly how Neil differs from those who are the easy targets of his "nastiness." He works dilligently—perhaps a bit too dilligently—at making a virtue of having no definable values. The result is a reductive process that makes middle-class life mushroom into such grotesquery that even a Neil looks attractive by comparison.

Roth's strongest suits have been a sense of naturalistic detail and an ear for the flavors of native speech. In "Goodbye, Columbus" the twin virtues occasionally pull in opposite directions. Short Hills, for example, is an Edenic world where sweat is the result of grueling tennis matches rather than hard work. Sport abounds—from the swimming pool to the driving range to the basketball court—along with the more literal "fruits" of the leisure class: cherries, plums, watermelons. In fact, Roth uses food as an index that keeps the Klugmans forever separated from the more affluent Patimkins. At dinner, Aunt Gladys wonders if Neil is "going to pick the peas out is all? You tell me that, I wouldn't buy the carrots" while at the Patimkins' "fruit grew in their refrigerator and sporting goods dropped from their trees." For an author who could claim, in 1961, that "Small matters aside—food preferences, a certain syntax, certain jokes—it is difficult for me to distinguish a Jewish style of life in our country. . . ,"[1] it is these "small matters" that dominate the texture of "Goodbye, Columbus." Here people *are* what they eat.

Moreover, the naturalistic nuances (the food on people's tables, like the garbage in their pails, is revealing stuff) quickly escalate into heavyhanded satire. The Patimkin refrigerator—both a haunting reminder of less prosperous days in Newark and a visible indication of their new suburban credentials—would be more at home in the world of Andrew Marvell's "The Garden" than a game room in Short Hills. The quasi-epical catalogue of luxuriant fruits ("There were greengage plums, black plums, red plums, apricots, nectarines, peaches, long horns of grapes, black, yellow, red, and cherries, cherries flowing out of boxes and staining everything scarlet.") suggests Marvell's world of "nectarine and curious peach," but, more importantly, the lushness that ensnares a Klugman is akin to the Edenic world that trips up the protagonist in Marvell's poem.

To be sure, Marvell brought his metaphysical imagination and the conceits associated with such poetry to bear on an Adam with no Eve in sight. Klugman, on the other hand, finds himself in Brenda's clutches from the very beginning. Radcliffe girls, I suspect, do not find the portrait of their "classmate" to be either flattering or accurate. Like most fictional college students, Brenda's liberal-arts education is reduced to that easiest of all "liberations," a swinging flipness, a shallow sophistication. The following exchange is particularly revealing:

> "You know," Brenda said, "you look like me.
> Except bigger."
> We were dressed similarly, sneakers, sweat socks,

1. Philip Roth, "Commentary Symposium," *Commentary*, XXXI: 4 (April 1961), 350.

khaki Bermudas, and sweat shirts, but I had the feeling
that Brenda was not talking about the accidents of
our dress—if they were accidents. She meant, I was sure,
that I was somehow beginning to look the way she
wanted me to. Like herself.[2]

If life with Aunt Gladys and Uncle Max is too con-
fining (ethnically "Jewish"), the Patimkins sound the
same "responsible" notes in another key. Neil, of
course, seeks a personal freedom as elusive as it is
romantically impossible: He has made of selfishness
an existential point of honor. That he is beginning to
look like Brenda and that he might, one day, act like
Ron Patimkin fills him with justifiable horror. After
all, Ron is an unabashed glutton at the Patimkin dinner table, a "crew-cut Proteus rising from the sea"
and, worst of all, the lover of recordings by Andre
Kostelanetz. Neil may be a snob, but, then again, Ron
more than deserves the condescension. He will follow
his father's game plan into the world of Patimkin
sinks as faithfully as he had obeyed his coaches at
Ohio State.

Neil, on the other hand, finds his "job," as opposed
to a "career," at the public library a joyless business
at best. The bureaucratic stink is, alas, everywhere.
His fellow librarians are infected with the function-
ary's mentality: as cautious as they are petty, as regu-
lation ridden as they are mean spirited. Surrounded
by the tyrannical wielders of small power, Neil finds
solace in an alter ego of his own choosing—a Negro
boy who makes daily pilgrimages to the library to look
at "heart" books. Here, of course, the mispronuncia-
tion of "art" strikes Neil as charming (one wonders if

2. Philip Roth, *Goodbye, Columbus* (Boston: Houghton
Mifflin Company, 1967), p. 70. (Hereafter page numbers appear
in parentheses.)

9

he would have reacted the same way had his Aunt Gladys made the error). In any event, the young Negro boy is a perfect candidate for a partner in some bookish secret sharing. The boy discovers Gauguin, and Neil finds himself protecting both the boy and the expensive reproductions from unworthy adults who would check it out. The shy Negro thus serves as a point of reference when the garish world of the Patimkins threatens to become unbearable. Also, his alternating bravado and uneasiness at the library is a mirror image of Klugman's own behavior in the alien ground of Short Hills.

Their fusion is achieved symbolically, in a mythopoeic dream full of echoes to Leslie Fiedler's *Love and Death in the American Novel*:

> The dream had unsettled me [Neil]: it had taken place on a ship, an old sailing ship like those you see in pirate movies. With me on the ship was the little colored kid from the library—I was the captain and he my mate, and we were the only crew members. For a while it was a pleasant dream; we were anchored in the harbor of an island in the Pacific and it was very sunny. Up on the beach there were beautiful bare-skinned Negresses, and none of them moved; but suddenly *we* were moving, our ship, out of the harbor, and the Negresses moved slowly down to the shore and began to throw leis at us and say "Goodbye, Columbus. . . goodbye, Columbus. . . goodbye. . ." (74)

A number of critics have pointed out that the Yiddish word *klug* means "clever," although Irving Howe insists that Neil is neither very clever nor much of a man,[3] and one is reminded of the Yiddish curse "*A*

---

3. Irving Howe, "Philip Roth Reconsidered," *Commentary*, LIV: 6 (December 1972), 70. Subsequent references to

klug af Columbus!" (A curse on Columbus!), which was a commonplace of the Lower East Side's nongolden streets. Roth, of course, pleads ignorance where matters Yiddish are concerned, but "new worlds" abound in "Goodbye, Columbus" nonetheless—from Ron Patimkin's shmaltzy record about Columbus, Ohio, to Neil's mythic dream about exotic islands and old-style explorers.

What Neil eventually bids a scornful goodbye, Ron embraces with a vengeance. In a story that risked becoming vulgar—as well as being about vulgarity—by piling up cheap shots (at one point Mrs. Patimkin quizzes Neil about Martin Buber's synagogue affiliation: "Is he *reformed*?"), the infamous wedding of Ron and Harriet pulls out all the stops:

> The husbands [of Mrs. Patimkin's twin sisters], named Earl Klein and Manny Kartzman, sat next to each other during the ceremony, then at dinner, and once, in fact, while the band was playing between courses, they rose, Klein and Kartzman, as though to dance, but instead walked to the far end of the hall where together they paced off the width of the floor. Earl, I learned later, was in the carpet business, and apparently was trying to figure out how much money he would make if the Hotel Pierre favored him with a sale. (106–7)

"Goodbye, Columbus" is filled with easy targets (suburbia in general; the Hadassah in particular), all too easily hit.

But sophomoric swipes aside, it was the ersatz psychology of "Goodbye, Columbus" that reduced Roth's vision to the merely glib. As a post-Freudian, he vacillates somewhere between the half serious and the self-

---

Professor Howe are to this brilliant, but somewhat carping, analysis of Roth's strengths and weaknesses.

consciously playful. The result insures a certain amount of "victory" in advance: Read the story's resolution through Freudian prisms and you miss the satiric point; deny the implications of "accident" and you miss even more.

Yet, for all the straining Roth does in behalf of shocking sexuality—Brenda and Neil playing musical beds or hide-the-diaphram—the story is now dated, even old-fashioned. For one thing, rewriting the saga of a rebellious protagonist who swaps a possessive woman for an ill-defined freedom puts Roth in very good, if "traditional," American company. But for all the charges and countercharges (Brenda's "forgetfulness" is more than matched by Neil's relief that the affair, at last, is over), "Goodbye, Columbus" transcends its conventional plot as a summer romance marooned on the rocks of autumn. For the moment at least Neil's floating anxieties have found an anchor worthy of his undivided contempt. And when he bids Brenda a final goodbye, he not only kisses off a Jewish-American princess, but all the Patimkins everywhere: "I . . . took a train that got me into Newark just as the sun was rising on the first day of the Jewish New Year. I was back in plenty of time for work" (136). Now the "sun also rises" for hard-boiled Jewish boys who have learned to mimic Jake Barnes rather than suffer along with Robert Cohn.

Neil Klugmans are made rather than born, and in a story like "The Conversion of the Jews," Roth suggests something of the process. Its protagonist, Ozzie Freedman, is a childish prototype of Alexander Portnoys. Here the principal battleground is a religious school and the "principle" combatants are Ozzie Freedman, whose forte is posing embarrassing questions, and Rabbi Binder, who can only respond with pedestrian answers. Their names, of course, are highly suggestive, especially if one reads the story in the symbolic shorthand of a wish-fulfilling dream. Ozzie has established a sizable reputation as a troublemaker before the story proper begins. Not that he is unruly in the usual sense of the word; Rabbi Binder could handle that problem. Rather, Ozzie is a pint-sized subversive, one who calls the basic tenets of Judaism into question. For example, Ozzie once wanted to know

> . . . how Rabbi Binder could call the Jews "The Chosen People" if the Declaration of Independence claimed all men to be created equal. Rabbi Binder tried to distinguish for him between political equality and spiritual legitimacy, but what Ozzie wanted to know, he insisted vehemently, was different. (141)

With a few more years (and quite a few more hangups) under his belt, Alexander Portnoy will shout much the same message at his parents. In "The Conversion of the Jews," however, Ozzie becomes a "freed man" via a fantasy that blends the dreams of a biblical Joseph with the interpretations of a Sigmund Freud. The literal level of the story fades gradually into the background at the traumatic moment when Ozzie screams "You don't know anything about God!" and Rabbi Binder responds uncharacteristically with an authoritarian slap. Ozzie bolts from the classroom of the synagogue to its roof, where his declarations take on the character of a rebellious id pitted against constraining superegos. Considered mythically, Ozzie emerges as an ironic Joseph, one whose dreams are filled with authority figures bowing before his will. Indeed, all the standard representatives of societal force are there—preacher, teacher, fireman, cop—and Ozzie, for the moment at least, reigns supreme:

> "Everybody kneel." There was the sound of everybody
> kneeling. . . .
>   Next, Ozzie made everybody say it [that God can
> make a child without intercourse]. And then he
> made them all say that they believed in Jesus Christ—
> first one at a time, then all together. (157, 158)

The story's title comes from a line in Andrew Marvell's "To His Coy Mistress": "And you should if you
please, refuse/ 'Till the conversion of the Jews." Roth's
vision combines a fantasized Day of Judgment with
a symbolic death wish. That is, Ozzie plunges into the
very fabric of his dream, "right into the center of the
yellow net that glowed in the evening's edge like an
overgrown halo."

Unfortunately, Ozzie's "triumph" is a fragile one
at best. Ozzie is as much a straw man for the forces
of self-righteous rebellion as Rabbi Binder is a convenient whipping boy for an insipid Judaism. For all
the hysterics, the "theological" questions Ozzie poses
are neither very tough nor, for that matter, particularly novel. In a richer story—"Defender of the Faith"—
Roth looks at the anguish of authority from the other
side of the coin. For Sgt. Nathan Marx a military identity, with its clearly delineated expectations and responsibilities, is uncomplicated in ways that his nearly
forgotten Jewish heritage can never be. John Wayne-
like characters are usually spared such existential
grief. Marx, however, finds that a training camp in
Missouri can be more wounding than battlefields.
When a goldbricking recruit sniffs out the chink in
Marx's professional armor, "Jewishness" becomes inextricably linked with vulnerability and victimization.

Let me quickly add that "Defender of the Faith" is
a complicated story, one easily misread by those who
judge fiction by the dubious yardstick of what is—or

is not—"good for the Jews." For such readers (and Roth has made it his business to attract many of them) "Goodbye, Columbus" is "indiscreet." Ostentatious Jewish weddings may be a fact, possibly even a vulgar one, but why advertise it to the *goyim*, why hang such dirty linen on the public lines? On the other hand, "Defender of the Faith" is not only indiscreet, it was downright unfair! To portray Jewish soldiers as connivers is a slur against all those who fought bravely against the Nazis, etc. Even Hollywood movies, which are always filled with microcosmic platoons containing a token black, an Orthodox Jew, a red-necked Southerner, a Midwestern farm boy, know better. In those grade-B scenarios the Jewish boy (with steel-wool hair and a Brooklyn accent) eventually earns the respect of the bigot who had ridiculed his Jewishness as "un-American." Moreover, when little Hymie dies during the third reel (mumbling barely audible Hebrew words), even the bigot is moved: "Ah don't reckon ah know what he's a-prayin', but ah reckon his God understans." Needless to say, this is not the story Roth had in mind, but it is, in large measure, what his readers had been conditioned to expect.

The very title of the story, "Defender of the Faith," is an ironic allusion to English sovereigns and an equally ironic comment about Marx and/or Grossbart. Marx is rudely plunged into all the ambivalences that accompany being appointed "defender of the faith" at Camp Crowder. Grossbart (who makes the "appointment") is, at best, a self-serving defender of the faith claimed by Fishbein and Halpern. In truth, Grossbart is a highly efficient barracks lawyer. At synagogue services, for example, "Grossbart's prayerbook remained closed on his lap" and when it came time to drink the Sabbath wine, "Grossbart swigged

15

in one long gulp, Halpern sipped, meditating, and Fishbein faked devotion with an empty cup" (171). Sergeant Marx—uncomfortable in a service he does not quite know why he bothered to attend—watches their antics from the back row and, at one point, imagines that he hears Grossbart cackle, "Let the goyim clean the floors!" He has, he realizes, been had.

The crux of the story revolves around the central question posed in *Goodbye, Columbus*: What are other Jews to me or me to them that they should expect—yea, even demand—preferential treatment? In different ways, both Roth and Marx anguish over the answer. The vulnerability creates a sensitivity (which is, I suppose, worthwhile) and a lingering inaction (which, as Hamlet discovered, is not). Grossbart, meanwhile, goes at the smallest opening with highly efficient can openers. He begins by referring to Marx as "Sir" rather than "Sergeant" and then moves through a litany of whining that includes an appeal to attend Friday night services, a request for kosher food, and finally the necessity of a weekend pass to attend a belated seder. Marx finds himself caught in the crunch between Captain Barrett's military ethic ("Who does more for the Jews, you [Grossbart] by throwing up over a lousy piece of sausage, a piece of firstcut meat—or Marx by killing those Nazi bastards?") and Grossbart's chauvinistic claims on behalf of Jewish solidarity (". . . we're the Messiah. Me a little bit, you a little bit . . ."). Grossbart becomes, in effect, the secret sharer of Marx's ambivalent Jewishness. His desperate appeals for special treatment ("Because I'm a Jew. . . I *am* different.")—always complicated by extenuating circumstances juxtaposed with the suspicion that he is more con man than religious martyr—tug at Marx in ways that are as unfair as they are effective. Obvious-

16

ly this is not the kind of situation dealt with in the army manual. Grossbart's whining makes that all too clear: "Ashamed, that's what you are so you take it out on the rest of us. They say Hitler himself was half a Jew. Seeing this, I wouldn't doubt it" (188). It is in speeches like this that the strengths of "Defender of the Faith" can be felt most strongly. An ear for the subtle nuances of diction is a rare gift, particularly in young writers out to prove that they, too, have read the classics. But with language stripped to its starkest rhythms, Grossbart and Marx thrust and parry about the heart's deepest needs in a way that shows Roth coming to grips with the very essence of complexity— that apparently sound positions can contradict one another. Granted, there is a considerable difference between Grossbart's eloquent appeals in the name of nonconformity (like Melville's Bartleby he knows the power of preferring not to) and his less-than-honorable motivations. Grossbart may be the stinker in Marx's scenario, but such characters are harder to develop than the term *stereotype* can suggest. Roth's technique here is to develop Grossbart in terms of the grotesque, stretching the inclination to hedge one's bets into a full-blown campaign strategy. His very name betrays the penchant toward such excess. And, yet, Grossbart's shotgun method scatters just enough pellets of "truth" (or, perhaps, seeming truths) to take a toll on Marx. The exterior barrage comes to personify everything Marx had imagined was hidden within the anonymous folds of his uniform.

In short, Marx is moved by Grossbart's heavy-handed tactics; a three-day pass is surreptitiously extended, and Grossbart & Co. will have their postponed seder after all. Or so Marx believed, believing in more than he had imagined possible. Such is the "faith" of which comic disappointments are made. Grossbart's much-vaunted seder with all its rationales stretching back to Egyptian bondage, ends in a bad joke. Promised a piece of gefilte fish, Marx gets a Chinese egg roll instead. After all, as Grossbart later explains, there was a mix-up about the dates ("I just reread the letter. *Next* week."), and they took "second best." Here Roth is on more congenial turf, exploiting surface ethnicity rather than the deeper rhythms of Jewish life.

The egg roll is, to mix a metaphor, the final straw. What had been moral paralysis changes to outrage and humiliation: "I couldn't stop the fury. It engulfed me, owned me, till it seemed I could only rid myself of it with tears or an act of violence" (197). Marx exorcizes the ghost of Grossbart by means of both—there is violence and there are tears in his self-styled revenge. In effect, Marx *becomes* Grossbart or at least utilizes Grossbart's manipulative skills against him. The result makes Marx the dispensator of poetic justice, the genuine (rather than inauthentic) "defender of the faith." When he reads the orders that had come down from C&A, Marx can hardly believe his eyes. Every trainee *except* Grossbart is scheduled to be shipped to a camp on the West Coast and from there to battlefields in the Pacific. Only Grossbart is destined for Camp Monmouth, New Jersey, and safety. As Marx puts it: "He had pulled a string and I wasn't it."

But Marx has learned the lessons that victimhood will teach. To be taken in by arguments about what a shared "faith" demands is also to know how such fallacious arguments work. Victims can and often do turn into victimizers, especially when they have been scorned. And so Marx pulls a few "strings" of his own, this time in reverse:

> "This may sound crazy, Bob, but I got a kid here on
> orders to Monmouth who wants them changed. He had
> a brother killed in Europe and he's hot to go to the
> Pacific.
>
> ". . . he's a Jewish kid, so he thought I could help
> him out. You know." (198)

The ironies here are savagely Sophoclean, a way of
converting Grossbart's forward energy into a boom-
eranging circle. As Marx tells the outraged, foiled
goldbricker, the seemingly vindictive act was done
"for all of us." Here, of course, the *all* reads "all Man-
kind," rather than "all Jews." Grossbart was more a
defender of his own advantage than of faith; Fishbein
and Halpern merely provide a convenient rationale.
But Marx, the protagonist of Roth's story and its moral
center, has had to grapple with that amorphous thing
called heritage. He opts (as the story demands he
should) for larger definitions of responsibility and the
complex fate each of us shares as a human being. In
the barracks all men prepare themselves for what looms
ahead:

> With a kind of quiet nervousness, they polished shoes,
> shined belt buckles, squared away underwear, trying
> as best they could to accept their fate. Behind me,
> Grossbart swallowed hard, accepting his. And then,
> resisting with all my will an impulse to turn and seek
> pardon for my vindictiveness, I accepted my own. (200)

An ambivalent note perhaps, one that strains just a bit
at credibility. It is not easy to imagine a Grossbart ac-
cepting a world without strings to pull. One might
realistically see him scurrying to the pay phone, desperately dialing one more call. And Marx's guilt is as
hard to swallow as his overly poetic sense of Fate.
Destiny joins forces with moral earnestness to make
for neatly packaged endings all around.

Authority has yet another face in "Eli, the Fanatic," a story that critics generally agree is the most impressive in *Goodbye, Columbus*. If Nathan Marx acts from a subtle mixture of emotions, Eli Peck is plunged into a situation where the nuances come in distinctly minor keys. Peck does not have to deal with the existential crises that war presents; he instead lives in the stifling safety of an affluent suburb. For the citizenry of Woodenton, New York, only that which is "different" constitutes a threat to the hard-won gains assimilation has made. As a community built from virtually interchangeable parts, the old animosities between Jew and gentile are finally disappearing. But Rabbi Tzuref and his disquieting yeshivah disrupt the comfortable arrangement.

Peck is a lawyer caught between his anxious clients ("Tell this Tzuref where we stand, Eli. This is a modern community . . .") and a growing realization that there are "laws" and Laws, zoning ordinances and what exile teaches people like Tzuref. Unlike the cloying Grossbart, Tzuref is a grotesque of a very different color, one marked uncompromisingly "Jewish." That is, Tzuref may be protean, hard to pin down with points of law, but his purposes speak to values the Jews of Woodenton have long ago forgotten:

> "The law is the law," Tzuref said . . . "And then of course"—Tzuref made a pair of scales in the air with his hands—"The law is not the law. When is the law that is the law not the law?" He jiggled the scales. "And vice versa." (251)

The image of tipping scales is a useful synecdoche for the story as a whole. Justice, both poetic and legalistic, ultimately involves a balancing of empathy, a sharing of alternative life styles, even a switching of clothes.

Like Sergeant Marx, Eli Peck is a gingerly "defender of the faith," this time defined as the ability (even *necessity*) of minority groups to melt into the fabric of mainstream America. As Peck's carefully argued letter to Tzuref puts it:

> It is only since the war that Jews have been able to
> buy property here, and for Jews and Gentiles to live
> beside each other in amity. For this adjustment to be
> made, both Jews and Gentiles alike have had to
> give up some of their extreme practices in order not to
> threaten or offend the other. (262)

Peck's argument makes sense in much the same way that the "law is the law." Consensus reality is on his side; the Old World yeshivah of Tzuref seems out of time, out of place.

Ironically enough, that is exactly the premise that Roth's story tests out. Consensus authorities aside, it is Peck rather than Tzuref who suffers an identity crisis. The tension pits a vaguely Hassidic mysticism against a satirized Freudian psychology. Surrounded by lives lived with what Thoreau called "quiet desperation" and its noisier manifestations ("I had a sort of Oedipal experience with the baby today," Peck's wife writes in a kitchen note about her unborn child), Peck is on the verge of a breakdown. The cocktail chatter about neuroses may be the dominion of suburban chic, but it is deeply unsatisfying for the individual neurotic. In Woodenton, even a mildly examined life turns out not worth the living.

Tzuref's old-fashioned Orthodoxy catapults Peck out of secular time, out of a house filled with TV dinners, sling chairs, and floating anxieties. In sacred time there is only the eternality of Sinai and the Commandments divinely revealed there. Peck may be inarticulate about their appeal and uncertainly unable to list what, exactly, the ordinances are, but he would swap his torts for Tzuref's Torah nonetheless.

Interestingly enough, the characteristic posture of the American-Jewish writer has been one of flight from the Hassid and all he represents. The reasons may have varied widely, but the end result was the same. The tightly drawn ideological lines that pitted Orthodox fathers against free-thinking sons gave way to half-disguised folk tales and irrational superstition as convenient indicators of the "religious." If the Hassid —with his disdain for American mores—was considered, first, an unsavory "greenhorn," he became a political reactionary in the decades that followed. Rather than the Yahweh of biblical memory, it was the new-found Trinity of Freud–Darwin–Marx that was carried into battle against more modern Philistines. In short, the Hassid came to symbolize that last, nagging barrier to sexual freedom, socioeconomic progress and full credentials as a mainstream American. As one of Peck's constituents puts it:

> "There's going to be no pogroms in Woodenton, Right? 'Cause there's no fanatics, crazy people— . . . Just people who respect each other, and leave each other be. Common sense is the ruling thing, Eli. I'm for common sense. Moderation." (277–78)

And, yet, for all its initial difficulties, the battle for assimilation was a relatively short skirmish. The harder task of assessing that "victory" fell to contemporary American-Jewish writers like Philip Roth. What immigrant authors knew at first hand and what the next generation learned from their grandparents, contemporary authors were forced to learn about from textbooks and university seminars. This is particularly true where the figure of the Hassid was concerned. His outlines became increasingly "academic" as reality gave way to the need for an apt metaphor of the moral passion that would come to dominate American-Jewish fiction after World War II.

In "Eli, the Fanatic," the result makes for a better fiction than it does a representation of fact. For example, when Tzuref defends his assistant's strange—and all too embarrassingly public—garb by saying "the suit the gentleman wears is all he's got," Eli is driven to supply him one of his own. The makeshift conglomeration of Ivy-League clothing is as out of place at the yeshivah as the black caftan had been on Coach House Road. As Sol Liptzin points out: "the tale illustrated Roth's efforts to find his way back to Jewishness, whose negative aspects he depicted far too often," but it also revealed "his ignorance of the inner motivation and behavior of Jews."[4]

Granted, the mysterious gentleman in black who exchanges his Hassidic trappings for Eli's surburban uniform is hardly a convincing portrait of Orthodoxy. The laws of *shatnais*, which deal with forbidden blendings of fiber, would override such trading. Poetic license aside, the details of the story can only look rather silly to those acquainted with Hassidic life. Roth has obviously neglected his Sunday-school homework. On the other hand, the nearly Shakespearian device of the costume-switching strikes us as right *aesthetically*, what the story—if not a genuine Hassid—demands.

Eli not only exchanges his contemporary refinements for the mantle of history, but, more importantly, he assumes the psychic identity of his alter ego. In Con-

4. Sol Liptzen, *The Jew in American Literature* (New York: Bloch Publishing Co., Inc., 1966), p. 228.

radian fashion, he puts on the clothing of the secret sharer and attempts to achieve a spiritual kinship via mystical transference:

> The recognition took some time. He [the Hassid—in Ivy-League drag] looked at what Eli wore. Up close, Eli looked at what he wore. And then Eli had the strange notion that he was two people. Or that he was one person wearing two suits. (289)

The story ends on this note of total substitution, as Eli completes the movement to that ambiguous level of myth where madness and clear vision remain suspended.

The stories in *Goodbye, Columbus* pit the Jews of stereotype against the more human ones we meet and are. In "Epstein," Roth deflates the going myth that Jewish husbands are as faithful as they are hardworking. "Why all the *schmutz*?" Theodore Solotaroff once asked him. "The story is the *schmutz*," Roth replied.[5] He was never more correct. *Schmutz*—literally "dirt" in Yiddish, but also suggesting the unsavory in general—is at the very heart of this sadly funny story. Lou Epstein is a restless, unfulfilled man. As he puts it: "What could he do? Does a man of fifty-nine all of a sudden start producing heirs?"

The answer to Epstein's rhetorical question is, of course, "No!" Men of fifty-nine do not have children, at least not in the stories written by twenty-six-year-olds (with, say, an I. B. Singer it might have been another story altogether!). But they do have affairs, even if—or, perhaps, because—they are Jewish.

When Epstein "accidently" (perhaps voyeuristically) watches his nephew seduce a neighbor's daugh-

5. Theodore Solotaroff, "Philip Roth: A Personal View" in *The Red Hot Vacuum* (New York: Atheneum Publishers, 1970), p. 312.

ter, his thoughts turn from assorted troubles to the tolls that time takes on his wife Goldie's body. What was "once small and tight, now could be poked and pulled"; "instead of smelling a woman between his sheets he smelled Bab-O." But at least in 1927 they were "handsome people," not like his daughter Sheila (a fat girl with pimples and a "social conscience") and her folk-singing beau. Epstein's "problem" is akin to the one that so disoriented Eli Peck, although, here, the crisis hits a generation later. Perhaps the closest equivalent to Lou Epstein that more recent times have produced is television's Archie Bunker, the frustrated bigot who sings "Those Were the Days" every Saturday night.

Ida Kaufman provides an alternative of sorts to the disappointment Goldie has become. While Goldie continues to divide all of humanity into "poor" and "nice" eaters ("Recipes she dreams while the world zips," muses Epstein), Ida Kaufman turns out to be good for a much-needed laugh. Unfortunately, she also seems to be good for a "rash," and the resulting "inspection" scene between the naked Goldie and the embarrassed Epstein is Roth at his unmerciful best.

Epstein's comic rash, like the sad comedy of Epstein's life, is hardly the element to create a tragic moment. He may have had an affair with Ida, but he is not afflicted with venereal disease because of it. Justice and guilt feelings remain very far removed; Epstein is no Job! Through it all Roth has a good laugh at the expense of middle-aged flesh. But it is a smart-alecky, cruel laughter. Epstein suffers a heart attack, and Roth's readers suffer through an ambulance reconciliation. "You have something that will cure what else he's got—this rash?" Goldie pleads. "So it'll never come back," the doctor replies, but somehow, we could care less. Even the satirically drawn Patimkins earn more of our sympathy and concern. Which is to say, "Epstein" is a "dirty story" not because it does dirt on sex but because it fulfills Lawrence's definition of the pornographic by doing dirt on life.

Finally, a word about the least interesting story in *Goodbye, Columbus*—"You Can't Tell a Man by the Song He Sings." Newark remains the milieu, but, here, the fictional landscape has "Joe McCarthyesque" overtones. Politics replaces the socioeconomic concerns that had made Roth such a shrewd observer of American-Jewish life; rather than bagels, we have ominous file cards, witch-hunting committees. The faults in this story foreshadow Roth's sophomoric approach in *Our Gang*, as his self-righteousness eliminates moral dilemma, convictions replace nagging doubts.

The story itself is told in retrospect, as a narrator recalls a freshman high-school class called "Occupations." In a highly significant detail their teacher, Mr. Russo, is described as a "square-shooter," the sort of guy who "would not go out the front door of the classroom to sneak around to the back door and observe how responsible we were."

Much of the plot revolves around the strange friendship between the unnamed Jewish narrator and the would-be tough guy, Albert Pelagutti. With a fascination about gentile freedom that prefigures an Alexander Portnoy, Pelagutti is described as having ". . . done all the things I, under direction, had not: he had eaten hamburgers in strange diners; he had gone out after cold showers . . ." (235). However, for all the comic dimensions of Pelagutti at bat (his lavender undershorts hanging a good three inches beneath the outer gym shorts, his sleeveless undershirts, even the incongrous "thin black silk socks with slender arrows embroidered up the sides"), the story is an object lesson in the subtle differences between appearance and reality. Pelagutti is the lovable villain of the piece, a leader of classroom revolutions that marked him as "no Capone, this was a Garibaldi!" For example, Pelagutti conducts an unscheduled "group sing" (including "Don't Sit Under the Apple Tree" and "The Star-Spangled Banner") in an effort to wrest control from Mr. Russo's gentle hands.

Later, Roth's protagonist finds himself involved in horseplay that suddenly becomes more serious. When a cafeteria window is broken, the crowd (including Pelagutti) scatters, and our narrator finds himself on the proverbial carpet. There he learns the first lesson in the realism that had made a Pelagutti run: Now his name and his "crime" are neatly typed on a school filing card, one the principal claims "will follow me through life."

But in a heavyhanded reversal years later, the Kefauver Crime Committee does not unearth a Pelagutti; rather, a McCarthyite investigation reveals that Robert Russo had once been a Marxist "while attending Montclair State Teachers' College circa 1935." As the narrator discovers in one way—and Russo in another—"You Can't Tell a Man by the Song He Sings." Time plays the cheat with such stories. Roth's sustained exercise in political satire, *Our Gang,* builds in many of the same liabilities, the same ragged edges that history makes.

And, yet, with all its limitations, *Goodbye, Columbus* was an impressive debut indeed. A National Book Award, an instant visibility, and an unending warfare with the guardians of official Jewish morality were only a part of the picture. There was genuine talent as well. That the talent has not yet quite managed to fulfill itself is what the rest of this study is about.

FIRST—CHILL—THEN STUPOR:
THEN THE *LETTING GO*

WITH the publication of *Letting Go* in 1961 Philip Roth began a period of extended experimentation that, generally speaking, has been as disappointing as it probably was necessary. By "experimentation" I do not mean to dredge up those exotic resonances we associate with the avant-garde, but to suggest that Roth started pouring his "new wine" into some very "old bottles." The short story had been a perfect form for the flip postures of *Goodbye, Columbus*. With *Letting Go*, no less a craftsman than Henry James was invoked as Roth tried his hand at that difficult, nearly un-American form called the "novel of manners."

The result was a sprawling, largely unresolved affair that strained for significance on one hand and dazzled with small brilliances on the other. Part of the blame must rest on Chicago, a locale Roth writes about with an unrelieved grimness. Part of the problem is built into its context as an "academic" novel, especially for a writer like Roth who finds it hard to strike a balance between satirical aloofness and passionate self-righteousness. But these are small matters, not necessarily fatal to a novel with as much sense of disarming detail and localized vision as *Letting Go* has. The important flaws lie deeper, at a level where plot gives way to disconnected threads and moral complication resolves itself in sheer weariness.

Letting Go opens with a revealing letter to the novel's protagonist, Gabe Wallach, from his mother. It is both a deathbed confession and the first in a long series of "letting go's." Rather than the "prerogative allowed normal dying people" (instructions, final wishes, etc.), she, instead, accepts the collective blame for their family's grief: "Whatever unhappiness has been in our family springs from me." Gabe, surely an avatar of Roth himself, reads Henry James ("words of heroes and heroines tempting one another into a complex and often tragic fate") and vows that he will "do no violence to human life, not to another's, and not to my own." On such a note—either principled detachment or flat-out selfishness—wavers the tension between "hanging on" and "letting go."

The action of *Letting Go* begins in the predictable shabbiness that is both the nostalgic memory and the grim reality of graduate-student life. That is, apartments furnished in early Salvation Army, cars on the edge of collapse, threadbare coats, and embattled spirits. Gabe Wallach, however, is spared whatever ravages genteel poverty might exact from the human spirit; instead, he is beleaguered by long-distance calls from his father and bombarded by checks he seldom bothers to cash. Like a Henry James character leisure is his vaguely unhappy lot, the cross he bears with dilettantish grace.

Paul Herz, on the other hand, is a graduate student etched in more familiar terms. He "was forever running . . . and forever barely making it":

> Once, shopping for some bread and milk, I saw him nearly break several of the major bones in his body at

29

the entrance to a downtown grocery store. The electric
eye swung the door out at him just as he had turned,
arms laden with packages, to watch a cop stick a
ticket under the single wiper of his battered, green,
double-parked Dodge.[1]

To Gabe, Paul Herz seems to find a perverse pleasure
in "saying to the world: Woe is me." All the small,
daily sufferings that the flesh can endure increase his
spiritual standing in the hyper-sensitive academic community. Such a fellow *must* be more "sensitive," better
than the fat souls who surround him. Besides, Paul is
a would-be writer, presumably suffering for the art
he presumably will make.

And, finally, there is the frail, but defiant Libby.
As Paul affects the tragic postures appropriate to one
who has sacrificed "all" in the cause of commitment,
Gabe's sympathies gradually shift to the equally beleaguered wife, Elizabeth (Libby) DeWitt Herz. The
marriage may have united a marginal Catholic (Libby)
with a marginal Jew (Paul), but the respective families
were violently opposed: "Once Jew had wed Gentile
wounds were opened—in Brooklyn, in Queens—that
were 'unhealable.' " Paul plods on with the energy of
quiet defiance, while Libby rails against the unending
mediocrity of her life in ways that foreshadow the
Lucy Nelson of Roth's next novel, *When She Was
Good*, as well echoing Flaubert's *Madame Bovary*.

And, yet, for all of Libby's affinity with the restless
Emma, it is her correspondence to Isabel Archer of
James's *The Portrait of a Lady* that Roth belabors in
Letting Go. Significantly enough, Gabe lends Libby a
copy of the novel (with the equally significant letter
from his mother tucked inside), wondering if "perhaps

1. Philip Roth, *Letting Go* (New York: Random House,
1961), p. 4. (Hereafter page numbers appear in parentheses.)

offering the book to be read in the first place had been my way of offering the letter to be read as well." Later, one wonders if he had not been really "offering" himself.

My argument thus far runs the risk of making Roth seem more self-consciously "literary" than he probably is. As an unrelenting critic of artificially imposed symbolism when he taught courses in creative writing at the University of Iowa, Roth insists, rather, that the best fiction is the result of hard, concrete surfaces. *Letting Go* presents a convenient vehicle for releasing the "gripes of Roth." In effect, the novel splits Roth's psyche into two separate, but unequal parts: the wise-guy that is Gabe Wallach and the sad-sack called Paul Herz.

Academe *per se* merely provides the backdrop: Paul rushes off to teach depressing night-school classes at a nearby school; Gabe discovers that even unambitious (gentlemanly?) teachers of literature must attend boring committee meetings. But student papers —to say nothing of the students themselves—are conspicuously absent. By this I simply mean that the issues of *Letting Go* are to be found in moral complexity rather than pedagogical tension. Gabe, Paul, and Libby form the central triangle of such entanglement, moving from one side of the desk as students at the University of Iowa to colleaguehood at the University of Chicago.

Something of Gabe's principled noncommitment is foreshadowed in his brief, half-hearted, undemanding relationship with Marjorie Howells. In a romantic revolt from all that Kenosha, Wisconsin, stands for, Marjorie finds with Gabe the exotic promises announced by "Halvah and Harvard and Henry Wallace." Gabe, of course, is amused by the cachet gentile midwesterners traditionally have placed on the urban, liberal, "hip" Jew. On the other hand, when she moves into his apartment, lugging her omnipresent bottle of Breck shampoo, an Olivetti typewriter, an electric frying pan, and the *Oxford Book of Seventeenth Century Verse*, he does not resist. As Gabe wisecracks: " 'Oh, Margie, I am your Trotsky, your Einstein, your Moses Maimonides.' And that foe of Luther and the Middle West asked, 'Was that his last name?' "

Letting Margie go is comparatively easy, especially when juxtaposed against the ambiguous "relationship" he develops with Libby Herz. If Gabe is Margie's muddled notion of the liberated Jew, to Libby he is the Grail Knight who can redeem her from Wastelandish sterility. In a scene chocked-full of Freudian allusions, Paul leaves—presumably to work in his office—while Gabe ministers to the bedridden Libby:

> When I came back into the bedroom again, Libby was sitting in her bed just as I had found her when I'd entered earlier. Only now she looked even more completely the victim of her undiagnosed illness. . . .
> I walked over and handed her the water. She took only a sip and then handed it back. I felt the touch of both the cool glass and her fingers. I sat down on the edge of the bed and without too much confusion, we kissed each other. We held afterwards, but only for a second. (56)

The scene reverberates throughout the novel, in Gabe's gingerly steps toward a commitment he did not seek or especially want, in Libby's fierce devotion to some better life that eludes even her fierce will and, finally, in Paul's sense of that justice which would match Libby's infidelity with his own. One hundred pages after Gabe and Libby kiss innocently and "let go" well short of consummation, the psychological destiny that had brought the potential adulterers together is explained in a significant flashback: Paul had "wished" the event; Gabe is as much *Paul's* romantic savior as he is Libby's. "Take Libby," Paul writes, driven by equal doses of frustration, jealousy, and abject despair. As a struggling novelist, he cannot force the ragged edges of life into the borders of art; as a failing husband, he can no longer love; as a spiritual man, he cannot believe.

Still, the final words of Paul's journal suggest otherwise: "*Libby* confessed. Wallach kissed her. She sobbed for an hour. Nothing more happened. Nothing. A precious girl. A precious girl. I'm ripping all this up. Every word. Start over. Try!" In Paul's case, however, "trying" is largely a matter of defining his familial relationships. Marrying Libby DeWitt was the very cause of crisis; resolution must necessarily be postponed until his father dies and Paul can effect a separate peace with the tangled threads of his Jewishness. Pain becomes a holding pattern, one that threatens to drown Paul in self-generating "hoit." Although Gabe can handle the competing tugs of *his* parents—their abiding love evidences itself in dental hygiene and mystical nuttiness on his father's part and the "taste and reason and powerful self-control" on his mother's —the tighter-lipped Paul is nearly destroyed by the same pressure. A man whose life had run on the smoothest of schedules (applications completed in the fall; scholarships granted in the spring), Paul finds himself untracked by the consequences of his love for Libby. Suddenly all the old securities are risked with a girl, as his parents point out prophetically, who is both Catholic and sickly.

Into Paul's rather maudlin and predictably dreary psychodrama (at one point his mother weeps: "My baby, he could read the mileage off the speedometer before other kids could even talk. What's happening

to my baby?"), Roth inserts two memorable characters by way of comic relief: Uncle Asher, a Bohemian
failure, and Uncle Jerry, a more conventional one. Presumably these minor figures can make "sense" where
parental hysterics cannot. But as Stanley Cooperman
points out: "Asher is what Alexander Portnoy aspires
to be: the Jew without Judaism; that is, without moral
imperative."[2] Even more significantly, he is, in Cooperman's words, "a painter who mocks art, a lover who
mocks love, an intellectual who mocks intellect, a
moralist who mocks morality, a 'survivor' who finds
no joy in survival." Paul's extended conversations with
this free spirit rotting away in its "freedom" frame his
moral problem and the terms of its resolution. While
Paul is on the brink of marrying Libby, Asher provides
him with a stark lesson in self-styled "history," one
that goes well beyond mere cynicism: "What are you
going to grow up to be, a canner of experience? Let it
flow, let it go. Wait and accept and learn to pull the
hand away. *Don't clutch!*" (82). Much later, his life
in tatters, his father dead, and the Asheresque attractions of New York outweighing his responsibilities to
Libby, Paul suddenly pulls back, convinced for the
first time that his lot *is* the morally committed life. At
the cemetery he "felt himself under a wider beam,"
moved by a moment as mystically religious as Asher's
is nihilistic.

If Uncle Asher's crude wisdom boils down to a
realization that "Ass is no panacea," Uncle Jerry provides its sentimental counterpart: "The heart, Paul,
knows. It cost me half a lifetime to learn such a simple
fact." But life is too complex for needlepoint maxims

2. Stanley Cooperman, "Philip Roth: 'Old Jacob's Eye'
With a Squint," *Twentieth Century Literature*, XIX: 3 (July
1973), 210.

—whether they be expounded by the Epstein-like Jerry or the Portnoyesque Asher.

In fact, Paul is bombarded with "good advice" on all fronts, from a well-meaning family out to spare him "grief" to equally well-meaning colleagues who know the curious ways of the academic world. Gabe Wallach has a foot in each camp. He offers Paul the use of his car in graduate school and, later, is the prime mover behind Paul's being offered a job at the University of Chicago; he pays a fence-mending visit to Paul's parents and ultimately arranges the all-important adoption for the Herzes. Without Paul the saga of Gabe Wallach could not sustain even a thin novel, much less one that rambles for some 600 pages.

Moreover, the Paul-Libby-Gabe triangle tests Roth's growing interest in the spidery nets human hearts spin. Money functions as the binding cement. In a realistic novel readers expect a sense of how much a loaf of bread costs and how characters earn their ready cash. *Letting Go* is filled with moments when price tags intrude upon idealistic dreams, when bank accounts (or the lack of them) signify all. In such a world even an eight-dollar hairdo at the Carita Salon looms as a foreboding detail. Libby insists on preparing such a face before facing Paul's family, while Paul can only wonder "Eight dollars!", amazed that the undergraduate Libby could be so bourgeois after all. Hadn't he taught her about the Good, the True, and the Beautiful? Where does beauty-parlor extravagance fit into *that*? "I can't afford stuff like that, Libby. We're going to have to live a frugal life. A sensible life" (98).

Alexander Portnoy will spin similar dreams with the "Pumpkin," imagining a tight little academic ship (paperback books in orange-crate shelves, a modest stereo set, a collection of classical records, etc.), able to skim over philistine seas. In Paul's case, genteel poverty is the drab badge of courage the sensitive life demands. But what sounds good on the rationalizing tongue often cloys in the unfed stomach.

Gut realities have a way of intruding in *Letting Go*. Acting, in effect, on Uncle Jerry's desperate faith in being "loved" and ultimately "touched," Paul and Libby decide to get married—and by a rabbi to boot! Unfortunately, the angry words of Rabbi Lichtman burst yet another bubble: "I marry Jew and Jew. . . . That's all." Lichtman is tough (*too* tough for many readers), but he sets the stage for a world where choices have consequences, where one cannot follow secular and religiously ordained motives simultaneously.

Finally, there is the rather heavyhanded scene at the restaurant as Paul and Libby agonize about a possible abortion. Once again rude interruptions, in this case Libby's unwanted pregnancy, are played against the continuing backdrop of makeshift economics. Forced to abandon temporarily (?) his academic dreams, Paul works in an automobile plant where, loser that he is, he soon injures his hand. Disregarding the symbolic aspect of the incident—whether it signify castration or merely an inconvenience for one who fancies himself a writer—Paul's efforts to hold the perilous situation together are matched by Libby's last-ditch attempt to eke some money from the De-Witts. However, as her father sees it: "My obligations, Mrs. Herz, are to sons and daughters, family and Church, Christ and country, and not to Jewish house-wives in Detroit." Shades of Lichtman in another key! "Desperate" would be a charitable way of describing the situation as they sit in a familiar delicatessen pondering what alternatives lie at the end of their dreamy tethers. And it is at such a point that Roth cannot resist the joke from ambush, the relevant detail brought in at an oblique angle:

> Solly rapped with a knuckle on the counter. "What's a matter, you kids can't decide what movie? See *Ten Commandments*—it's got a beautiful message."
>
> "Thanks, Solly, no," Paul said. "Libby's got a cold."
>
> "How about a piece of boiled chicken?" Solly asked. (122)

All of the narrative concerning Libby's abortion is presented in a flashback. Meanwhile, the forward motion of *Letting Go* takes a distinctly academic turn.

Gabe, for example, soon discovers that the Beowulf of dreaded classes in Anglo-Saxon is not the only monster lurking about academia. Critics can be even more frightening, particularly if they come at literature like the chairman of his department, John Spigliano. Convinced that *creative writers* (a term Spigliano uses with smug derision) are apt to be "too personal about literature" and, as if that were not bad enough, "most of them are without any real critical system," Spigliano is an easy target for the testy Paul and the testier Roth. Battle lines are drawn early, and department meetings given over to tedious discussions about various philosophies of grading—the forces of Life (Paul) pitted against the ogres of Style (Spigliano); those who admire a witty turn of phrase (Gabe) against those who insist on correct punctuation (McDougall).

Like a good many other "academic" novels, talk *about* students far outweighs their actual presence; cocktail parties, rather than classrooms, are where the real comedy of manners takes place. It is at such a party that Gabe Wallach meets Libby's struggling counterpart, Martha Reganhart. Unlike the soporific

Margie Howells, Martha has wit and a savvy sense of who she is.

Unfortunately, Gabe's insistence about an "uncomplicated life" forecloses in advance many of the possibilities of developing a relationship. Gabe uses Martha more as a badly needed aspirin than an object of love; he relies on her when a Thanksgiving with his father becomes unbearable or when he feels regret about trying to seduce a female colleague. Although Martha *says* that "nobody has to marry me . . . Nobody ever has to feel obligated . . .," Gabe mistakes the ease of "shacking up" with its inevitable consequences. But, for the moment, what could be more convenient than a woman who proclaims exactly what he wants to hear?

Gabe soon discovers that it is the Martha Reganhart, divorced mother of two small children, who speaks louder and more clearly. Sid Jaffe, a successful attorney, had offered her both marriage and assorted securities in one large sweep. Martha, instead, opts for the more exciting Gabe Wallach. But it is the very tenuousness of their relationship that accounts for the running battles about how rent should be split (Gabe retains his apartment, largely for "symbolic" value; Martha, on the other hand, loses a rent-paying boarder when Gabe moves in). At a disastrous dinner party with the Herzes, everything imaginable goes wrong: Martha decks herself out in Bohemian garb (complete with what Gabe calls her "Humanities II sandals"), while Libby comes on like a "child saint about to be lifted onto the cross." The oppulence of their roast beef offends Paul and Gabe's seven-dollar wine infuriates Martha. The evening ends, as it must, in a shouting match.

Paul and Libby leave in a huff, but there are no

straight lines leading away from such tightly inter-twined lives. Hasty exits lead, inevitably, to agonized returns. Martha's life is aptly described as a "circle" ("and if it ends where it begins, what is that? What's next?") and the phrase applies with equal force to the novel as a whole.[3] Doubling back through a network of fathers and sons, husbands and wives, lovers and loved ones is that contradictory motion we call attrac-tion–repulsion. The Martha who made such eloquent promises about an unobligated life becomes, some forty pages later, the desperate Martha who screams: "Oh Gabe, . . . I want you to marry me or give me up. I'm too old to screw around like this." Moreover, Gabe finally realizes that Libby had expected to be seduced, that he "was supposed to come along and rescue her!"

Gabe suffers from that modern malady called the blocked heart. As he puts it: "I'm no social worker. I'm tired of meddling in people's lives!" But to cause no other human being pain (i.e. remain uninvolved) makes for a better principle than an actual possibility. The child Paul and Libby so desperately need is a good case in point. Bitter memories of the Detroit abortion haunt Paul and Libby as their marriage crumbles against the cold winds of Chicago. At one point Gabe impatiently shouts: "Then give her a child. Have a child!"—without realizing that Libby's diseased kid-neys make such easy solutions impossible.

Adoption is, of course, one possibility, but pre-sumably even that alternative is denied to couples with mixed religious backgrounds. At this point Roth raises the decible level (his characters rant in ways that a

3. That is, the novel begins with a letter from Gabe's mother and ends with a remarkably similar letter from Gabe to Libby. In both cases, recognition and guilt go hand in hand. Structurally, the novel has come an ambivalent full circle.

Henry James would probably find uncivilized), and the essence of Isabel Archer gets lost in the translation to Libby Herz. By this I mean, there is a considerable gap between the young woman who dreamed of Spode china and the full-fledged neurotic who blows up at an investigator from the adoption agency. Even more significantly, Libby stumbles across Fitzgerald's *Tender Is the Night* and finds a fellow sufferer in Nicole.

The remainder of *Letting Go* is designed to set a number of unresolved situations at peace. In terms of sheer plot structure, Roth knits Gabe and Martha with Paul and Libby. They become, in effect, more Conradian "secret sharers," linked by bonds that lie deeper than individual rationalization can touch. Martha contributes the name Theresa Haug, a coworker at the Hawaiian House restaurant who, in turn, contributes the baby Libby and Paul "adopt"—this time with the amiable Sid Jaffe as the legalistic go-between. Granted, the adoption is not quite kosher, but, then again, Theresa is having an illegitimate child and Libby's behavior with a representative from an agency has made a more conventional adoption impossible. Martha, on the other hand, lets her children go (with Gabe as the overriding rationale), only to lose her lover to highbrow ennui and her son to a melodramatic accident (his older sister pushing him out of a bunkbed in what must be the most telegraphed, overwritten section of this ponderously overwritten novel).

Markie's death drives Martha back to Sid Jaffe's patient arms while the death of Paul's father drives him back to the synagogue. Libby finds a book entitled *The Wonder of Life* and contentment in grating potatoes for Chanukah latkes. Even Gabe temporarily abandons his father's advice ("Don't interfere!") and becomes, instead, the "Mad Crusader" of the book's penultimate chapter. Theresa reveals to Sid Jaffe that she had been married throughout her pregnancy—sensing both revenge and a financial windfall all in one diapered package—and Gabe springs into action. As some critics with a bent for religion and literature have pointed out, that his full name is Gabriel, that he "announces" the child to the childless couple, that he saves it from "foreign" clutches, all make for highly symbolic resonances.[4] Perhaps they are right.

But, as Martha points out with less symbolism and more precision: "Sid Jaffe happens to be a fine man. He's not jelly either." Gabe may be quasi-heroic as he faces Harry Bigoness (Theresa's cuckolded husband), but he cannot shake off the more subtle "hoit" of his Oedipal shackles:

> The circumstances of his father's union [remarriage] seemed to render him impotent. When he had the rights, he did not seem able to muster the power; when he had the power, he did not know if he had the rights—which washed away what power he had. (530)

Power, particularly where human relationships are concerned, is what *Letting Go* is all about. Paul simultaneously abandons the illusion of getting his Ph.D. and/or becoming a "writer," opting, instead, for a less competitive job teaching high school. Only types like Spigliano survive in academia. As for Libby, it no longer matters; happiness is feeling "Jewish," complete with aching wrists from grating potatoes and a daughter named Rachel. Even Gabe's father is no longer the lonely man on the other end of a long-

4. Glenn Meeter, for example, in an essay for a series on "contemporary writers in Christian perspective" (*Philip Roth and Bernard Malamud*, Grand Rapids, Michigan: Wm. B. Eerdmans Publishing Co., 1968) suggests all these and many more examples of Roth's essentially "religious" concerns.

distance call; he has found Fay Silberman and the possibility of "fun" in his old age.

Only Gabe is left to drift as uncommitted at the end of the novel as he was at the beginning. If Libby is a pale copy of the Jamesian heroine, Gabe bears more than a little resemblance to those American innocents like Christopher Newman who hide out abroad. As Gabe's letter to Libby, the conclusion of the novel, puts it:

> . . . It is only kind of you, Libby, to feel that I would want to know that I am off the hook. But I'm not, I can't be, I don't want to be—not until I make some sense of the larger hook I'm on. (630)

Letting Go ought to have been the sort of novel to clear the air, produce cathartic effects for its author. By this I mean, with a wide range of native tensions off his chest—and onto paper—the work that followed should have been less shrill, less chest-thumpingly adolescent. Unfortunately, it was not.

MADAME BOVARY IN THE AMERICAN HEARTLAND

Rᴏᴛʜ's next novel, *When She Was Good* (1966), was a conscious effort to prove he could write about non-Jews in non-Jewish settings. At that time, mulling over old wounds was either too painful or too exhausting for an author already beginning to feel the fickle stings of criticism. The reception of *Letting Go* had been downright cold or, at the very least, full of sober reappraisal. To add to Roth's misfortunes, Henry Roth's reissued novel *Call It Sleep* (originally published in 1934) had turned Philip, almost overnight, into "that *other* Roth."

Although I belabored the Jamesian influences on *Letting Go*, they are largely matters of overall vision and moral texture rather than the shape and ring of individual sentences. One could hardly confuse a typical passage from *The Ambassadors* with the gritty surfaces of *Letting Go*. In a similar fashion, when Roth turns his attention toward the Midwest, it is a land seen through the prisms of Flaubert's *Madame Bovary*. To be sure, Flaubert's aesthetically distanced tale of a woman consumed by illusions and trapped by circumstance is very portable indeed. Lending libraries take their toll, whether located in French hinterlands or American ones. Like Emma, Lucy Nelson wants an ill-defined "something" that will stand in bold relief against what she already has. Flaubert's protagonist was lured by the excitement of Paris. With Lucy, it is the chance to be recognized for a superiority instinctively felt.

But the deeply felt sense of place that had sustained Roth's earlier novels is missing in *When She Was Good*. Novels like William Gass's *Omensetter's Luck* or Wright Morris's *Ceremony in Lone Tree* render the Midwest in an actuality of detail that for Roth becomes a matter of seeing life from at least two removes. Liberty Center is the Heartland as Easterners imagine and fear it will be. Once again the overarching concern is to show the American Nightmare lurking just on the other side of the American Dream. In *When She Was Good*, Roth sets about the business of unraveling the mixture of deterministic conditions and systematic illusions that produce a Lucy Nelson.

Granted, that the American female is portrayed as a castrating bitch is hardly an innovative fictional idea; such "monsters" have a cherished, even traditional, place in the American novelist's psyche. But Roth alters the usual ground rules by arming her with narrative perspective and a filtering consciousness. With the exception of the opening chapters, *When She Was Good* is Lucy's saga, told with what, at first glance, looks like sympathy. However, what her strident voice insists upon is more than countered by the soft whispers of Roth we hear underneath. The result is a darkling tale, one that pays off debts for the unhappy years Roth spent in Iowa and at the same time established him as the man able to put *Madame Bovary* into an American idiom.

The novel itself opens in a cemetery, as Willard Carroll pays a meditative visit to the family burial plot. Unlike Lucy, the dream of his life is "not to be rich, not to be famous . . .," but "to be civilized." What follows is a telescoped history of a time when his brand of rugged individualism could still work, when keeping one's grip on the promise of America was still possible. Hardy fathers abound in contemporary literature (one thinks of the well-preserved Dr. Adler in Saul Bellow's *Seize the Day*) almost as nagging reminders to their spineless sons. Although Roth will insist that the rule does not apply to Jewish fathers (see Jack Portnoy et al.), it is perfectly appropriate to portray the character of gentile Willard Carroll as aging patriarch–wise man.

One of Willard's most vivid boyhood recollections —a traumatic incident that foreshadows Lucy's fierce will—concerns his sister Ginny. At the age of seven he had watched the one-year-old Ginny suffering the ravages of scarlet fever. An old Chippewa squaw gives her a root to chew and, miraculously enough, Ginny seems cured. Before that fateful night he had believed, as Lucy would later, that "what someone had at first denied him would sometimes be conceded if only he looked into the other's eyes long enough for the honesty and intensity of his desires to be appreciated."[1] The key phrase here is "the honesty and intensity of his desires"; that is the very essence of Willard's innocent belief in the power of personal charm. Later that night, however, Willard's father discovers his son forcing the root into the baby's lips, and an absurd injustice replaces good intentions and well-meaning plans:

> "You—let her be, get away," and so, helpless, he [Willard] went off to his bed, and had, at seven, his first terrifying inkling that there were in the universe forces even more immune to his charm, even more remote from his desires, even more estranged from human need and feeling, than his own father. (5)

The incident is a synecdoche of the book to follow, a way of capsulizing the alienation and terror that afflict the citizens of the ironically named Liberty Center. It is also a lesson Lucy never quite learns.

In *When She Was Good*, the generations oppose each other with a vengeance: Willard Carroll leaves his father's world of Iron City for the "freedoms" promised by Liberty Center. There he becomes a postal clerk and struggles to keep his house and family in good repair—"not only to maintain the comfort of those who live with him yet, but the dignity of all too, such as it is."

By 1966 "those who live with him" include his

1. Philip Roth, *When She Was Good* (New York: Random House, 1966), p. 4. (Hereafter page numbers appear in parentheses.)

wife Berta, his daughter Myra, and his son-in-law Duane ("Whitey") Nelson. Although Berta remains the "strong-minded and respectable girl" he married, Myra is a bitter disappointment and Duane a solid down-and-outer. The blame for a younger generation's flabby moral fiber is placed on a sleazy bar called Earl's Dugout. Whitey's "tragedy" is that of potential forever unfulfilled, of good intentions drowning in bad circumstances and booze. Willard plods forward through a long history of downward adjustments, sadly remembering the little girl Myra was ("Always practising something feminine: crocheting, music, poetry. . . .") years after she has become the long-suffering justifier of her husband's lapsability.

Duane's life is a series of fresh starts, of "temporary" moves into Willard's protective care that turn out, on second glance, to be semipermanent. In 1934, it managed to "stretch out to sixteen years of living off the fat of another fellow's land, which wasn't so fat either"; in 1954 the old hopes that Duane will straighten out are rekindled once again: "In that whole so-called Dugout of Buddies there was probably never a man who was one-tenth the worker, or the husband, or the father that Whitey was—that is, when things weren't overwhelming him" (18).

In large measure, what "overwhelms" Whitey is his daughter Lucy. Surrounded by inferiors of every stripe, Lucy is a monument to the power of self-induced "specialness." Where others *ought* to be strong, they are weak, where they *ought* to recognize her virtues, they steadfastly refuse to do so. It is her curse to blossom unnoticed in the provincial gardens of Liberty Center.

It is here that the echoes of *Madame Bovary* are loudest. Not surprisingly, Lucy "protests too much" about her largely imagined superiority. For example, where Ellie Sowerby is concerned: "She was Ellie's superior in every way imaginable, except for looks, which she didn't care that much about; and money, which meant nothing; and clothes; and boys." Later, as Ellie's reluctant friend and a shy visitor at her house, she borrows a sweater from one of Ellie's bulging drawers. It turns out to be pure cashmere and the incident occasions a fancy bit of rationalization:

> . . . to change the cashmere for cotton, or even lamb's wool, would be to admit that she was indeed guilty of choosing it deliberately, when in actuality she had taken it in all innocence. . . It had nothing to do with being covetous and she would not give credence to any suspicion. . . . (90)

The scene is an effective foreshadowing of ever more elaborate self-deceptions to follow. Lucy's special brand of paranoia—unlike the sort that will be comically exploited in *Our Gang*—develops into elaborate defenses. It begins with an acknowledged guilt (she had chosen the expensive sweater "in all innocence") and escalates into uncharitable projection (the "suspicion" she simultaneously creates and attacks). Things like cashmere sweaters are not important anyhow, she exclaims, much like the unhappy fox eyeing the grapes in Aesop's fable or, say, any Fitzgerald protagonist insisting that he is having a "swell time" among the flappers. Because she is so insistent about "goodness," her tragic story has at least two faces—one that looks at the surrounding players and says, "Yes, Lucy, you *are* better than the rest of the lot!" while the other winks soberly and replies, "What an insufferable prig you are, Miss Nelson!"

With her penchant for absolutes, it is hardly surprising that orthodox religion—in this case, Catholicism—attracts the unhappy, highly vulnerable Lucy. Her parents seem an endless source of shame: from her mother's makeshift profession as a "piano teacher" (Lucy remembers "with a kind of dread" her classmates "waiting on the porch in warm weather") to her growing identity as "the kid whose father hangs around Earl's Dugout." As stories about the Nelson house make the schoolyard circuit, Lucy concocts excuses (her grandmother's "nap," for instance) to explain why her home is "off-limits" to her friends. But when even the newest girl there knows, Lucy resolves "from then on . . . never to tell a lie again, to anyone about anything."

Much of Lucy's subsequent "goodness" is the result of this crucial decision. Moreover, her "conversion" to a romantic Catholicism more her own making than Rome's (shades of Emma Bovary!) provides an index of difference between her own martyrdom and the insipid Protestantism of the other Nelsons. While working as a waitress at the Dairy Bar she meets the wayward Babs Egan and later her sensitive, victimized sister Kitty. What Lucy and Kitty share, of course, is a sense of sin (especially when evidenced in others) and an adolescent desire for personal purity. Best of all, Kitty did not go to Liberty High (where, presumably, the whispers about Lucy's family are deafening); rather, she attended the parish school at Saint Mary's. When Babs elopes—the final disgrace in a long series of sexual rebellions—Kitty meets Lucy, and both find their solace in "what Sister Angelica called 'Saint Teresa's little way of spiritual childhood.' "

To be sure, Lucy Nelson is no Saint Teresa, no Sister Angelica, indeed, no "angel." For all the romantic desire to live a similar life of submission and sentimental martyrdom, the self-righteous strain in

Lucy is too strong. In fact, she is more akin to the avenging God one associates with the Old Testament. When Lucy is "good," she fiercely expects others to be good as well, and when they are not, she becomes vindictive.

In one of the novel's more memorable moments, Lucy interrupts the flow of Saint Teresa's lifestyle for a more congenial solution of her own. Roth's tone here is devastating, suggesting the sizable gap between what people hope to be and what they actually are:

> So Lucy dedicated herself to a life of submission, hu-mility, silence and suffering; until the night her father pulled down the shade and up-ended the pan of water in which her mother was soaking her beautiful, frail feet. After calling upon Saint Teresa of Lisieux and Our Lord—and getting no reply—she called the police. (80)

The decision to call in the police (more efficient representatives of the superego than God) creates a breach that never quite heals. Instead, Lucy replaces an ethic of submission for one of vocal truth telling. Presumably, it is the *truth* that will set her free.

Roy Bassart, Ellie Sowerby's cousin, provides all the catalyst such a Lucy needs. In 1948 he had returned from the army, no longer a "boy" and not yet a man. Which is to say, he "didn't know what to do with his future, so he sat around for six months listening to people talk about it." His "interests" include drawing, a 1946 Hudson, and Hydrox cookies—not exactly what his parents consider the raw material for a future. The banality with which this type of subject infuses the book might be compared to John Updike's approach in *Rabbit, Run*. That is, like Rabbit Angstrom, the fading former basketball star gone somewhat seedy, Roy Bassart is thoroughly ordinary. Writing about such characters is a risky business, but Roth catches just the right flavor of gnawing discontent and inaction. Roy may be "bugged," but one suspects he is not going to do much about it. He is exactly the sort of G.I. whose well-meaning mother had once sent a package of toilet-seat liners with a card reading: "Roy, please use these. Not everyone is from a clean home." Now that he has "returned," Roy can count on even more "protection."

Nevertheless, Roy nurtures a sense of specialness not unlike Lucy's.

> . . . you lost your identity in a gang, and Roy considered himself a little too much of an individualist for that. Not a loner, but an individualist, and there's a big difference. (55)

Although a virgin, despite his hitch in the army, Roy thinks of himself as a crusty ex-G.I.: worldly, experienced, far above the current high school crowd. That he is kidding himself is only to say that his eventual marriage to Lucy has been fashioned in heaven. Never have two people so richly deserved each other.

To be sure, Lucy will later insist it was Roy who seduced *her* with his half-baked notions about "interruption" (a technique Roy had heard described in the Service), but it is hard to tell the deceivers from the deceived in *When She Was Good*. All the desperate, fumbling passion in the back seats of automobiles—generously punctuated by "Please?" and "No!"—makes it clear that Roth rediscovered the gold mine in crew-cut Don Juans long before the producers of *American Graffitti*.

With Lucy, however, Roy's "techniques" are more successful, although only after a frustrating courtship in which he begs his "angel" to "trust me, trust me."

Lucy does, and destinies of the flesh take over. Roy becomes a student at the Britannia School of Photography while Lucy enrolls at the nearby Fort Kean College for Women. Add the new-found freedom of Roy's apartment and frustration seems very much a thing of the past.

But the seeds of Lucy's discontent have already been sown. She is really Roy's superior after all. Granted, he "never tried to boss her around—except for sex," but, even there Lucy is confident she can control Roy. However, what she is really concerned about is that the relationship is developing too quickly —and with an inferior person!

Unfortunately, Lucy's unexpected pregnancy sidetracks thoughts about never "start[ing] up in the car" or of calling an abrupt "Stop!" to the sexual proceedings. To the school doctor—a more sympathetic man than Lucy imagines—she is a first-semester freshman in deep, but not uncommon, trouble. Lucy, on the other hand, waxes indignant about the cosmic injustice that would level her to the position of others:

> "I don't want to marry him. I don't want to lie to you.
> I hate liars and I don't lie, and that's the truth!
> Please, hundreds and hundreds of girls do what I did.
> And they do it with all different people! . . . But I'm
> not bad! . . . I'm good!" (41)

"Truth" is her magic talisman, the banner she hauls into battle against those too stupid to recognize her inherent virtue. What begins as a local observation ("But my family *is* terrible," she tells the doctor. "I don't think it—it's true!") quickly mushrooms into snipes at Roy, his family, the ineffectual doctor, and, finally, everyone. Not since Henry Thoreau exercised his Transcendental authority has an American character been so utterly convinced about individual rightness. Lucy's outbursts never risk a democratic vote, much less what consensus reality might affirm.

The tensions of *When She Was Good* are generated when others perceive a truth that is at loggerheads with Lucy's. The result makes for shouting in a brow decidedly lower than *Letting Go* but with much the same effect. At bottom the issue is power, a commodity Lucy envisions in uncompromisingly moral terms. As she puts it: "If only they'd say *no*. NO, LUCY, YOU CANNOT. NO, LUCY, WE FORBID IT." However, when they do not (or, perhaps, can not): "She had won. She could do whatever in the world she wanted—even marry someone she secretly despised" (150). And so she does. But the "victory" has, as it must, an ashy taste. Caught between wanting moral authorities and nipping them in the bud, Lucy becomes the architect of her loneliness.

What her parents and the Church could not provide is beyond the ability of a placid Roy as well. Their marriage begins and ends in a power struggle, which Lucy wins by default. From a cocky student at Britannia (a suspect institution at best, with equally "suspect," "pansy"-ish teachers) Roy becomes an assistant to Wendall Hopkins, the "society photographer" of Fort Kean. For all of Roy's initial, and terribly naive, enthusiasm, it turns out to be as mediocre a job as Roth's more sophisticated readers suspect it will be. After all, what sort of work could the "society photographer" of Fort Kean do, much less his "assistant"?

And, so, Roy drives the backroads of Kean County, photographing graduation classes for a man whose business "it turned out, was not out of the Fort Kean social register, but from the Board of Education, of which his [Hopkins's] brother was a member." Economic and moral squalor sets in quickly. With Roy's "creativity" systematically stifled, he counters with dreams of a private studio—complete with business cards printed by a firm in Cleveland. Lucy, on the other hand, merely resents her lot: the marriage, her husband, her child, the unfairness of it all. Roth paints a grim picture of marital "un-bliss" (shades of *My Life as a Man*), but one so grounded in the ordinary that even the constant bickering strikes us less as grotesque than all too true.

When Roy finally suggests "a sort of separation," the battle lines begin to shift from Fort Kean to Roy's family in Liberty Center. Uncle Julian Sowerby, it seems, has convinced Roy that Lucy is insane. The *real* confrontations are yet to come—not between the spineless Roy and the castrating Lucy, but between the straight-talking Julian and an increasingly desperate Lucy. The conflict reaches a crescendo at Fort Kean when Lucy accuses Roy of being a "pansy" and, in effect, excommunicates him from the moral universe she controls: "You are beyond hope. Beyond endurance. You are beyond everything. You can't be saved. You don't even want to be" (263). Roy counters by taking his son (whose choral refrain "I hate Mommy, her face is all black" sets the tone for the final showdown) to the safety of Liberty Center.

Lucy follows like an avenging, if somewhat disorganized, angel. To be sure, the long bus ride from Fort Kean must have been tiring, but Lucy bursts into the Sowerby home armed with righteous indignation nonetheless. After all, Roy had a "duty" to his wife and child; "he" had seduced her! But Julian is less than moved by Lucy's noisy theatrics and more interested in conferring upon her the ironic sainthood she has been seeking throughout the novel: "That's the saint you are kiddo—Saint Ball-Breaker. And the world's going to know it, too, before I'm through with you." The long night's battle is punctuated by frantic phone calls and equally frantic declarations about "innocence" until Lucy's paranoia dovetails into downright madness. According to Lucy, her father long ago deserted the family because he was "terrified of my judgment"; the Bassarts refuse to believe she is pregnant once again; even Daddy Will (Carroll) disappoints her in her hour of greatest need.

Convinced that the world is madness, Lucy grabs a letter from her father (written, significantly enough, from another in a series of many prisons) and trudges melodramatically into the night. Only organ music and audience "hisses" have been omitted. As Lucy freezes into the snow, her last thoughts ("For they are wrong, and you are right, and there is no choice: the good must triumph in the end! The good and the just and the true *must*—") sum up a life riddled with illusions to the very end.

Like the *Madame Bovary* on which her character is based, Lucy can never quite reconcile the life that ought to be with the life that is. Romanticism, particularly when it hardens into such firm convictions, is a deadly business. Emma and Lucy end as suicides, destroyed by self-created vanity. In this sense Lucy's theme for freshman English on Shelley's "Ozymandias" is truer (run-on sentence aside) than she had realized:

". . . 'Ozymandias,' which not only reveals the theme of the vanity of human wishes—even a king's—but deals also with the concept of the immensity of 'boundless and bare' life and the inevitability of the 'colossal wreck' of everything, as compared to the 'sneer of cold command,' which is all many mortals have at their command, unfortunately." (180)

LIFE INSIDE A JEWISH JOKE

PARTS of it had already appeared in *New American Review*, *Partisan Review*, and *Esquire*. Publicity about it appeared everywhere: on television talk shows, in newspapers and, of course, among indignant congregations of synagogues. The advance sales were staggering; rumors about what Hollywood was willing to pay for the rights dazzled serious writers and critics alike. It was 1969 and it seemed a sure bet that the decade would end with a literary bang. The book was, of course, *Portnoy's Complaint*.

But sensation has a nasty habit of leading us astray—to tedious discussions about the coexistence of serious art and high profits. In that sort of frenzy, the book itself can, and often does, get lost. *Portnoy's Complaint* is a prolonged *kvetch* (in English, read "complaint"), one nervously anchored to the analyst's couch. Unlike *Letting Go* or *When She Was Good*, it is the influence of the stand-up comedian (rather than the high-brow, sit-down writer) that is felt most strongly. And this is particularly true in the book's rhythm, it "blends" from one comic bit to another. Granted, literary allusions are sprinkled generously throughout (from *King Lear*, Yeats' "Leda and the Swan," Kafka and, of course, *Oedipus Rex*), but it is the unlikely combination of, say, a Myron Cohen and a Lenny Bruce that gives Portnoy's monologue its forward motion. Not since Salinger's *The Catcher in the Rye* had a novel been so readable, so "right" for its time and place. Portnoy was urbane, hip, swinging, irreverent, and cutely neurotic. And not since Holden Caulfield worried about the Central Park ducks and winter had so many readers identified so deeply with a character in literature. If Holden was the perfect embodiment of the innocent fifties, Alexander Portnoy was a prime candidate to be celebrated in the sexy sixties.

Such a book is, by definition, hard to pin down. Its very *title* works on at least three levels: as a "complaint" in the legalistic sense of an indictment handed down against those cultural forces that have created him; as a "complaint" in the old-fashioned sense of illness, one Dr. Spielvogel comically describes in clinical language as "A distortion in which strongly-felt ethical and altruistic impulses are perpetually warring with extreme sexual longings, often of a perverse nature"; and, finally, as a "complaint" in the more ordinary, "existential" sense of the word.

Alexander Portnoy, who is a thirty-three-year-old Momma's boy and New York City's Assistant Commissioner of Human Opportunity, finds himself at psychological loose ends at the novel's beginning. That his age is the same as Christ when crucified, that he protects the sacredness of every human opportunity (except, of course, his *own*) makes for intriguing possibilities. But *that*, it seems to me, is the critical point: *Portnoy's Complaint* is as filled with "possibilities"

56

as it is riddled with interior "contradictions." Portnoy would, no doubt, agree with the speaker of Walt Whitman's "Song of Myself":

> Do I contradict myself?
> Very well then I contradict myself,
> (I am large, I contain multitudes.)

The difference, of course, is that Whitman's poem is a hairy-chested celebration of his cosmic, largely imagined(?) selfhood, while Portnoy's systematic contradictions are the very heart of the confessional mode.

In this sense, Portnoy is closer to Leopold Bloom, the multi-faceted wanderer of Joyce's *Ulysses*. In the jumble of personality traits, the alternating currents of love and hatred, Portnoy is the protean teller of his own tragicomic tale. The book is simultaneously a confessional act and an attempt to exorcise lingering guilts. Both Bloom and Portnoy share that uneasy Jewishness that has become a fashionable mark of alienated modernity. But their respective contexts are worth mentioning, if only to temper the impulse toward total identification. Indeed, the differences between a Bloom and a Portnoy may be more revealing than the artificial similarities. To be a Jew in Dublin is to be a kind of walking contradiction, a joke *a priori*. Portnoy, on the other hand, grows up in that uneasy limbo between total assimilation and authentic Jewishness called Newark. Even he has trouble distinguishing the "truth" behind his compulsive needs to complain, to confess, to project guilt, to wallow in self-pity:

Could I really have detested this childhood and resented these poor parents of mine to the same degree then as I seem to now, looking backward upon what I was

from the vantage point of what I am—and am not?
Is this the truth I'm delivering up, or is it just plain
kvetching? Or is *kvetching* for people like me a
form of truth?[1]

Granted, Portnoy's fractured monologue comes all in
a rush, as if repression had made it impossible to talk
about these matters before. Still, his *kvetching* is a
"form of truth," especially if one sees it as the essential truth grossly distorted for comic effect. Portnoy's
self-lacerating wit bears at least some relationship to
traditional modes of Jewish humor. He knows, for example, how to beat a hostile world to the punch. Moreover, he undercuts himself with a relish that only those
infected with that sensibility we have learned to call
"black humor" can understand. Fantasy is its staple
ingredient. In Portnoy's case, the elusive truth is a
mixture of actual event and what the imagination can
make of it. Recurrent fears express themselves as
fantasized headlines in the Daily News and/or as
comic bits projected on the mind's inner screen.

For Roth, the technique was not only a congenial
way of writing, but at its best became a distinctive
style: what wowed them at one night's party was altered in his study the following afternoon. The raw
material of the *tumeler* could be metamorphosed into
high art. Sustaining such a "voice" throughout the
novel—a matter of refining language until it achieved
the illusion of colloquial speech—may at least partially
account for the book's enormous success and the film
version's dismal failure. In print even Portnoy's wild-
est, most obscene ranting has an appeal which is lost
when transcribed into another medium.

1. Philip Roth, *Portnoy's Complaint* (New York: Random
House, 1967), p. 94. (Hereafter page numbers appear in
parentheses.)

There are, of course, other "problems" with *Portnoy's Complaint*. For one thing, Portnoy has a viselike grip on the novel's point of view. The analyst's couch functions in roughly the same way that center stage did for the Barrymores. Other characters are relegated to secondary positions as straw men in the fractured chronology of Portnoy's shifting memories. But one begins to suspect that Portnoy, like Lucy Nelson, complaineth *too* much, that there is another side to his psychologically crippled coin, one that we are not hearing. At first glance the novel encourages easy identification—"Portnoy *c'est moi!*"—readers who are unaware that subtleties of tone may, in fact, be undercutting their "hero" at every turn. Others insist that the whole Jewish Momma–Jewish Son business is neither ethnically indigenous nor particularly unique; Italian mothers (or Russian ones, or whatever) share many of the same characteristics. And, finally, there are those who dismiss the portraits as patently unfair. For them nothing substantial had changed between *Goodbye, Columbus* and *Portnoy's Complaint*, except that the latest travesty was even "dirtier."

Portnoy begins his *shpiel* ("play") to Dr. Spielvogel with a sketch entitled "The Most Unforgettable Character I've Met." Unlike the uplifting stories that appear under that rubric in the *Reader's Digest*, however, Portnoy's version is darkly Freudian, an introduction to those determinants that have lowered him onto the couch. His mother is more a Borsht-belt fantasy than an actual person, the easy villain in this self-constructed Rorschach. As the capitol-S Superego, Sophie was so imbedded in Alexander's consciousness that "for the first year of school I seem to have believed that each of my teachers was my mother in disguise." Sophie is, of course, the Jewish-Mother joke incarnate, full of sardonic, but ultimately castrating wit. It is Sophie who looms over the terrified Alex "with a long bread knife in her hands" and Sophie who locks him out of the apartment when he is "bad." In her dual roles as "nurturer" and "devourer," she is the figure of the Mother outlined in anthropological studies like Robert Graves's *The White Goddess*. But most of all, she is "thorough":

> For mistakes she checked my sums; for holes, my
> socks; for dirt, my nails, my neck, every seam and crease
> of my body. She even dredges the furthest recesses
> of my ears by pouring cold peroxide into my head. (12)

Fears about the body's health, and the resulting, largely superstitious, remedies, are a legacy Portnoy both rebels against and cannot quite manage to shake. Given the omnipotent matriarch Sophie is, Alex seems driven to assert his masculinity via grotesque masturbations.

But genuine power is as confident as it is unquestioning. What Sophie knows unconsciously (without benefit of windy articles in *Partisan Review*), Alex can never understand by intelligence alone. His comic introspection may make him an attractive narrator to those afflicted by similar maladies, but it is the *un*-examined life that wields the psychological stick in *Portnoy's Complaint*. As Melvin Friedman is well aware, it is "Alexander Portnoy [who] requires psychiatric help, not his Jewish mother."[2]

Portnoy's father, on the other hand, provides a poignant model of all his darling son seeks to avoid. As Jack Portnoy's comic version of the Cartesian formula would have it: "I am a Jewish father; *ergo* (read:

2. Melvin Friedman, "Jewish Mothers and Sons: The Expense of Chutzpah," in Irving Malin, ed., *Contemporary American-Jewish Literature: Critical Essays* (Bloomington: Indiana University Press, 1973), p. 170.

No wonder) I am constipated!" Moreover, he is an insurance salesman, peddling the promises of security (an "umbrella for a rainy day") among the skeptical blacks of Newark. Long suffering as Sophie is constantly tormenting, Portnoy's father is the grumbling stoic, a man resigned to his inevitable fate as a chewer of Ex-Lax. He *provides*, but can find no "relief" for himself.

Portnoy's Complaint has a great deal in common with books like D. H. Lawrence's *Sons and Lovers* or James Joyce's *A Portrait of the Artist as a Young Man*. They are all versions of the *Bildungsroman*, novels that chronicle the "education" of a young protagonist. That the Oedipal complex, which so tortured Paul Morel (who doubles as both "son" *and* "lover"), is shared by Alexander Portnoy is as obvious as it is misleading. In a general sense Lawrence's novel is the prototype of those preoccupations that characterize much American-Jewish fiction: Freudian hatred of the father; obsessive love by and for the mother. But for all Portnoy's insistence that his parentage is the alpha and omega of his malady, socioeconomic factors (rather than purely psychological ones) also play a significant role. Portnoy belongs to that culture of sons for which immigrant Jewish parents worked. As Portnoy puts it: "where he had been imprisoned, I would fly: that was his dream. Mine was its corollary: in my liberation would be his— from ignorance, from exploitation, from anonymity" (8). Portnoy is, in effect, a scorecard of both the assets and liabilities of such a program. Groomed to succeed, he does. But what Norman Podhoretz calls the "small-print costs" of America's "brutal contract" are also there.[3] The curiously intertwining love and hatred

3. Norman Podhoretz, *Making It* (New York: Random House, 1967), passim.

Alex feels are no doubt matched by similar, albeit silent, emotions on the other end of the generational spectrum. Portnoy's swinging idiom may differ in degree from his father's, but they are very much alike in kind. What the former says with bile, the latter passes off with *schmaltz*.

It is easy enough to heap criticism on Alex's parents and their programmatic efforts to restrict his manhood, keep him forever the terrified little boy seeking praise. And, too, it is easy enough to rail at "this schmuck, this moron, this Philistine father of mine!" whose crime was to throw away copies of *Partisan Review* unread. But such adolescent postures (Why can't parents be more like professors? Like my favorite authors? Like ME!) begin to cloy in adulthood. After all, Jack Portnoy may not be a reader of high-brow journals, but he was the payer of expensive tuitions. Alex, of course, wants no truck with anything less rarified than high art. In this sense, he reminds one of Stephen Dedalus, a boy with equally strong views about the constraints imposed by Family, Church, and State. Alex joins his priggish precursor by refusing to serve the false idols in which he no longer believes:

> But I am something more, or so they tell me. A Jew. No! No! An *atheist*, I cry. I am nothing where religion is concerned, and I will not pretend to be anything that I am not! I don't care how lonely and needy my father is, the truth about me is the truth about me, and I'm sorry but he'll have to swallow my apostasy whole! (72)

In *Ulysses*, Stephen meets Leopold Bloom and learns those lessons about the human heart heady esthetes too often overlook. Alexander Portnoy has no such instructor. Moreover, he doesn't want one. His prolonged confession has a self-indulgent quality about it, as if "hoit" had become a comfortable part of the script. Chronology is arranged for maximum effect and twice-told tales are embellished by comic energy.

Life inside his particular Jewish joke is a way of stacking the cards, of controlling the impact of its pain. That Portnoy can talk so glibly about masturbation, impotence, and assorted perversions (real and imagined) suggests the difference between this book and those of Lawrence or Joyce. What they took with high seriousness, Roth reduces to the merely flip. The cunning of history is at work here. When Portnoy shouts "LET'S PUT THE ID BACK IN YID!" the effect dovetails Freudian jargon into the jazzy stuff of popular culture.

What the novel does provide is an encyclopedia of moments drawn from an American-Jewish ethos in its cultural death throes. One axiom strikes me as crucial here: At the very moment a tradition begins to question itself, to mount elaborate campaigns on behalf of cultural retrenchment, it is already in a stage of serious decline. Portnoy comes at the ragged end of a history that had sustained itself with dignity and now cannot. What he sees is the residue of a superstructure (ethnic indicators like "real Jewish jello" or Mah-Jongg), rather than its more meaningful substructure. In a book that militates against a complexity of characterization (substituting, instead, the stock figures of the skit and blackout) precious little sidetracks Portnoy's sweeping condemnations.

At one point, however, his father asks:

"Tell me something, do you know Talmud, my educated son? Do you know history? One-two-three you were bar mitzvah, and that for you was the end of your religious education. . . . Tell me, now that you are finished at fourteen being a Jew, do you know a single thing about the wonderful history and heritage of the saga of your people?" (62–63)

Fair questions all, although Jack Portnoy may not be the best person to ask them. For him the "saga of the Jews" is as much a cliché as are the terms of Portnoy's rejection. As Irving Howe shrewdly observes, what Portnoy *really* expresses is "the wish to sever his sexuality from his moral sensibilities, to cut it away from his self as historical creature." The result beckons a castration even more fearful than the one Sophie threatens. To live in an ahistorical anonymity is less a fashionable, liberating, dream than a foolish nightmare. Portnoy is, in fact, the most notorious spokesman for the special brands of schizophrenia and blindness that are the necessary by-products of such truncated lives. Even his ringing claim, "I am a human being!," rings as meaningless without a cultural context.

This much said, however, one must still turn to that vulgarization of culture that is Portnoy's unhappy lot. It is largely defined by an assortment of "Thou Shalt Not's!," some originating on Sinai, but most emanating from Sophie Portnoy herself. As Portnoy discovered in his childhood again and again, Jewish people do not "believe" in (a) Christmas (b) athletics in general (c) French fries (d) baton-twirling (e) hunting (f) etc. etc. At one point Portnoy recalls that, as a small child, he had "turned from the window out of which I was watching a snowstorm and hopefully asked 'Momma, do we believe in winter?' "

In the Portnoy household the world is divided neatly into that which is "Jewish" and the rest which is *"goyische"*:

> Because I am sick and tired of *goyische* this and
> *goyische* that! If it's bad it's the *goyim*, if it's good it's
> the Jews! Can't you see, my dear parents, from whose
> loins I somehow leaped, that such thinking is a trifle
> barbaric? That all you are expressing is your *fear*? (75)

Portnoy responds to the indoctrination with a solip-
sistic vengeance. And in that lonely world where he
alone is a "human being," he alternates between cas-
tigating the gentiles ("these people for whom Nat
'King' Cole sings every Christmastime, 'Chestnuts
roasting on an open fire, Jack Frost nipping at your
nose' ") and berating the Jews ("What in their world
was not charged with danger, dripping with germs,
fraught with peril?").

Rampant sexuality is Portnoy's weapon in his unending war against instilled repression and neurotic
fears about bodily functions. Not since Lawrence at
his wackiest has there been such phallic consciousness. That Portnoy suffers from a psychic impotence
seems exactly the wrong diagnosis for his chaotic
sexual behavior. From the imaginary Thereal McCoy
of his adolescent fantasies at the Empire Burlesque
House through his sordid history of private masturbations, semipublic displays on the 107 bus, and the wildly comic asset provided by Bubbles Girardi to his
pornographic dreams finally realized in Mary Jane
Reed (the Monkey), Portnoy appears hyperactive
rather than ineffectual. If the traditional *schlemiel*
was a cuckold or, at least, a kind of sexual sad sack,
Portnoy is his opposite—he scores big and often.

Freud's seminal essay "The Most Prevalent Form
of Degradation in Erotic Life" (which Roth borrows
wholesale as the title for a chapter about Portnoy's ill-
fated love affairs) suggests a partial answer: "Where

such men love they have no desire, and where they desire they cannot love." The underlying cause is, of course, the Oedipal conflict; an obsessive love for the mother turns subsequent women into versions of the Madonna or the Prostitute. As Portnoy reviews the respective trists with the Monkey, Kay Campbell (the "Pumpkin"), and Sarah Abbot Maulsby (the "Pilgrim"), his mother's hysterically capitalized warnings ring in his ears: "DON'T RUN FIRST THING TO A BLONDIE, PLEASE! . . . A BRILLIANT INNOCENT BABY BOY LIKE YOU, SHE'LL EAT YOU UP ALIVE!" (189). Portnoy has no trouble making dirty jokes from such "straight" lines, but the deep-seated guilts he rehearses never stray far from home.

In the case of the Monkey, an illiterate note to her cleaning lady ("dir willa polish the flor . . .") is at least as telling as her genital effusions about "Leda and the Swan." Even the notorious Molly Bloom did not make such glaring errors, and, to Portnoy, they matter deeply. He may be a professional defender of the downtrodden, but he is also not above a bit of snobbishness: "This woman is ineducable and beyond reclamation. By contrast to hers, my childhood took place in Brahmin Boston" (206).

Kay Campbell, on the other hand, is "hard as a gourd on matters of moral principle, beautifully stubborn in a way I couldn't but envy and adore." Best of all, *"She never raised her voice in an argument."* Unlike the middle-class screamers of *When She Was Good*, the Campbells are gentiles at their most genteel. When Portnoy visits their Midwestern, Norman-Rockwellesque home during a college vacation, he realizes, for the first time, that the English language can be *"a form of communication."* Things are otherwise in Newark, New Jersey. But the "polite" can also be the "lifeless," the bland, and Portnoy prefers those special revenges all paranoids gleefully imagine:

> ... if someone starts in with "the pushy Jews," or says "kike" or "jewed him down"—well, I'll jew them down all right. . . . I will shame them and humiliate them in their bigoted hearts! Quote the Declaration of Independence over their candied yams! (224)

Portnoy's worst fears are unrealized, but when Kay thinks she is pregnant, Portnoy thinks she will convert. When she refuses (with that soft-spoken determination that is *her* heritage), Portnoy erupts into "The Temper Tantrum Kid" (with all the shouting that is *his* lot as the spoiled "nice-Jewish-boy" he actually is).

And, finally, there is Sarah Abbot Maulsby, the Pilgrim. Her WASP credentials are even more imposing than the Pumpkin's had been: New Canaan, Foxcroft, Vassar. As a member of the House subcommittee investigation into the television quiz show scandals, Portnoy had attacked people like "Charlatan Van Doren" (the archetypal ur-WASP) with all the zeal of an Old Testament prophet. Miss Maulsby is thrilled by the energy of Portnoy's rough edges. But, finally, she too is *too, too. . .*

> Then there were the nicknames of her friends: there were the friends themselves! Poody and Pip and Pebble, Shrimp and Brute and Tug, Squeek, Bumpo, Baba— it sounded, I said, as though she had gone to Vassar with Donald Duck's nephews. (233)

All these abortive relationships can, of course, be chalked up to his tragicomic Oedipal complex. But the "hoits," it seems to me, run deeper than Portnoy's independent study in Freudian jargon can explain. Guilt is the special energy that makes a culture of sons like Portnoy possible. What he resists, in short, is the fatherhood that is both his destiny and his deepest fear. At one level of consciousness, he desperately wants "to grow up to *be* one of those men"; at another, he is afraid that he will become an avatar of his constipated father.

But in all fairness to the much-maligned Jack Portnoy, some of the novel's richest moments involve intimacies Alex remembers with a "hoit" very different from his comic slandering of Sophie. Granted, "whacking off" was (is?) too much fun to forget, but there were also "Walks, walks with my father in Weequahic Park on Sundays that I still haven't forgotten." While a Sophie can be simply stereotyped by an insistence that her "biggest fault" is being "too good," Portnoy's father is as complicated as he is long suffering. This aspect of *Portnoy's Complaint* brings it closest to the vision of Lawrence's *Sons and Lovers*. To imagine the authoritarian father "killed," replaced by a younger, more vigorous son is only part of the total picture; mothers (who, of course, cannot be "hit") ultimately trouble their sons much more. For all his human weaknesses (at one point Portnoy realizes, sadly, that his father is no "King Kong" Charlie Keller), Jack Portnoy projects as much quiet warmth as he does noisy *kvetching*.

If perversion is Portnoy's ambivalent response to American-Jewish life, Israel alters the situation as radically as it exhausts it comically. There even the bus drivers and policemen are Jewish; now the ongoing battle between the *goyische* world and the Jewish one no longer makes any sense. There, there are no *schikses*! They have been replaced by Naomi, a militant Israeli as tough in her Marxism as she is confident about her Jewishness. ". . . a Jewish Pumpkin! Portnoy

happily declares I am being given a second chance."
We, of course, know better. Impotence—what he will
later tag as "Monkey's Revenge"—remains Portnoy's
seriocomic fate.

But, more importantly, Naomi's tough-minded assessment of Portnoy's problem (in passages that prove
that Roth can, indeed, give an adversary position equal
time) suggests yet another face of the ubiquitous Sophie. She cuts through his pathetic whining with the
sharp edge that statehood—rather than comic "exile"
—saves for its wayward Jewish sons:

> "You seem to take a special pleasure, some pride, in
> making yourself the butt of your own peculiar sense
> of humor. . . . Everything you say is somehow always
> twisted, some way or another, to come out 'funny' . . .
> In some little way or other, everything is ironical, or
> self-deprecating." (264)

Has she, perhaps, hit Portnoy's confessional nail on
the head? Perhaps. But Roth knows full well how valu-
able such built-in criticism can be. It beats his critics to
the punch by alternating the distances he keeps from
his nervous protagonist. Portnoy is, at best, a vehicle by
which Roth controls the various "hoits" (however
exaggerated) of his own childhood.

And, yet, Naomi's words speak to the book's limitations nonetheless. *Portnoy's Complaint* is a *minor*
classic, "minor" in that it chooses to examine a highly
selected segment of human experience. Such rambling,
first-person narrative may be the stuff of a brilliant
tour de force, but it also has a way of exhausting the
possibilities a "thicker" novel would exploit. In a
very real sense, the novel itself disappears into the
"gags" and standup comedy that had provided its initial structure.

Indeed, "exhaustion" seems the perfect note on

which to end a discussion of this novel about psychic exhaustion. For all the zig-zag motion of Portnoy's continuing "complaint," what he presents is a guide to the "new *kvetching*" that characterizes the "new steerage":

I am not in this boat alone, oh no, I am on the biggest troop ship afloat . . . only look in through the portholes and see us there, stacked to the bulkheads in our bunks, moaning and groaning with such pity for ourselves, the sad and watery-eyed sons of Jewish parents, sick to the gills from rolling through these heavy seas of guilt—so I sometimes envision us, me and my fellow wailers, melancholics, and wise guys, still in steerage, like our forebears—and oh sick, sick as dogs, we cry out intermittently, one of us or another, "Poppa, how could you?" "Momma, why did you?" and the stories we tell, as the big ship pitches and rolls, the vying we do—who had the most castrating mother, who the most benighted father, I can match you, you bastard, humiliation for humiliation, shame for shame. . . (117–18)

Portnoy's Complaint is obviously the big winner in such a contest. It is a book that had to be written as much as it is the book that Roth had to write. As Portnoy bravely tears off the "Do Not Remove Under Penalty of Law" tag from his mattress and prepares to die with the bravado of a Humphrey Bogart ("while I lived, *I lived big!*"), the self-destructive monologue comes to an end (*im*ploded, as it were), and his analyst can, at long last, begin. Circular and systematically nonconclusive, *Portnoy's Complaint* laid out all the psychic pieces in a rush of comically verbal pyrotechnics. More importantly, it was the culmination of an urban, American-Jewish idiom that remains Roth's most congenial turf. He would not return to it until

My Life as a Man and, then, with a bitterness that made
Portnoy's complaint look like kid stuff. But *Portnoy's
Complaint* will survive—even one day transcend—the
assorted noises that have surrounded it. Because, for
better or worse, with this book Roth provided both a
chronicle and an epitaph for those times, that place.

THE MADNESS OF BEING "SENSIBLE"

SARDONIC wit is never at a loss for subject
matter these days; we live in times so absurd that it
is no longer necessary to read ponderous essays by
French intellectuals. The evening paper provides plenty of material in the unlikely event that the normal
events of the day do not. But this avalanche of human
folly is as much a curse as it is a blessing to the writer
of contemporary fiction, particularly if he has the
satirical bent of a Philip Roth. In the years following
Portnoy's Complaint it became increasingly difficult to
find a congenial home for his sizable verbal talents. The
grotesquery of the world chipped away at what a literary imagination might conceive, always threatening
to outdo in life what one had patterned in art.

In Roth's case, the late sixties took a fearful toll.
His next books were pitched on that shaky ground
called the playful gimmick. For a writer without his
reputation, the results, no doubt, would have been
fatal. For Roth, however, even the slimmest straw can
lead to a darkly comic drowning. A decade earlier Sal-

inger discovered that short stories like "Franny" and "Zooey" could be marketed as a thin, wide-margined book. Roth used the same ruse in *Our Gang* (1971) and *The Breast* (1972).

Our Gang was written in the white heat of indignation and outrage. To call Roth's grasp of politics "puerile" would be like equating a temper tantrum with sophisticated diplomacy. But in the context of 1971—with the war in Vietnam still raging and American citizens still deeply divided about its moral justification—critics tended to respond to the righteousness of his position rather than the artfulness of his book. Granted, novels are never written in a cultural vacuum; they always contain some residue of the social environment, such as the baggage of special interest groups and competing claims about what the "representative" consists of. Novels pinned to a volatile political climate merely render the problem exasperating.

A post-Watergate rereading of the novel is even more fascinating than reading it during the days when Nixon dictated our foreign policy. What some were quick to dismiss as cranky paranoia in 1971 has surfaced as a highly prophetic reality four years later. If anything, Roth's outrageous parody of Nixon is not outrageous enough for the postimpeachment era. Such are the risks the political satirist runs in our time.

Our Gang takes Nixon's position about abortion (San Clemente, April 3, 1971) as a convenient starting point. Here, for the record, is the genuine article:

> . . . UNRESTRICTED ABORTION POLICIES, OR ABORTION ON DEMAND, I CANNOT SQUARE WITH MY PERSONAL BELIEF IN THE SANCTITY OF HUMAN LIFE—INCLUDING THE LIFE OF THE YET UNBORN. FOR, SURELY, THE UNBORN HAVE RIGHTS ALSO. . .

And here is Trick E. Dixon, the protagonist of Roth's exercise in *extension ad absurdem*:

And let me make one thing perfectly clear: I am not just talking about the rights of the fetus. I am talking about the microscopic embryos as well. If ever there was a group in this country that was "disadvantaged," in the sense that they are utterly without representation or a voice in our national government, it is not the blacks or the Puerto Ricans or the hippies or what-have-you, all of whom have their spokesmen, but these infinitesimal creatures up there on the placenta.[1]

A comedian like Mort Sahl is not alone in realizing the comic potential of evening newspapers; Philip Roth knows how to extrapolate on a well-chosen passage with relentless energy. The bromides of political rhetoric make a virtuoso performance like *Our Gang* both possible and a bit too easy. By resorting to this type of structure, he is being sophomoric and self-indulgent.

Roth has picked epigraphs from Swift and Orwell to set the tone of outrages of his own to follow: Phrases like the "sanctity of human life" obviously mean one thing when the subject is abortion and quite another when it involves the war in Vietnam. Faced by such absurd contradictions, Roth strikes back. What if Lieutenant Calley had committed an abortion? In a news conference "troubled citizen" (allegorically, Roth himself) puts it this way:

CITIZEN: . . . What if Lieutenant Calley gave her an abortion without her demanding one, or even asking for one—or even wanting one?
TRICKY: As an outright form of population control, you mean?

1. Philip Roth, *Our Gang (Starring Tricky and His Friends)* (New York: Random House, 1971), pp. 12–13. (Hereafter page numbers appear in parentheses.)

73

CITIZEN: Well, I was thinking more along the lines of an outright form of murder. (9–10)

Granted, outrage may *seem* to be the only response one can make to double-think of this sort, but Swiftian satire is more than highjinks. In this sense, the best satire is a cool medium, one that makes control absolutely essential. To turn a Richard Nixon into a "Trick E. Dixon"; a John Kennedy into "John Charisma"; San Clemente into "San Dementia" takes no great talent. If stand-up comics like David Steinberg haunted the wings of *Portnoy's Complaint*, *Our Gang* contains the echoes of an impressionist like David Frye. It is easy to lampoon Nixon, and Roth does not hesitate to take some predictable, or to be less charitable, cheap, shots in the process:

As always, I want to make everything as perfectly clear to you as I can. That is why you hear me say over and over again, in my speeches and press conferences and interviews, that I want to make one thing very clear, or two things, or three things, or as many things as I have on my agenda to make very clear. (94)

By pushing ever so slightly on the artifice of such rhetoric, Roth, in effect, pulls the White House down. A few well-chosen chinks in Mr. Nixon's armor are all the opening really necessary. To be sure, the cunning of history will record otherwise. The man who immortalized the phrase "I want to make one thing very clear" kept some things very hidden indeed.

Roth's technique in *Our Gang* results in a series of loosely connected sketches rather than a novel per se. What Roth apparently wants to test here is how far one can unwind the absurdist string tied to Nixon's actual words. That Roth pushes beyond those limits that might have made for an amusing essay in a magazine like *The New Yorker* is a testament to his Blakeian faith in wisdom lying just the other side of excess. *Our Gang* quickly degenerates into pure experiment, a kind of spontaneous writing that allows a moral imagination the chance to run free. If premise A is patently absurd, what about its implications in terms of B? And, then, what about AB or C or ABC or D, ad infinitum, ad nauseum. With something like Swift's "A Modest Proposal" as a working model, the logic of *Our Gang* is as airtight as it is crazy. When absurdity is raised to yet a higher power, it becomes an infernal machine all its own, one built from calculus turned desperately playful.

President Dixon sets Roth's version of the domino theory in motion by declaring himself the protector of lives yet unborn. The result becomes a wildly comic (shrewdly calculating?) scheme to give them the vote as well:

> Here, at long last, we have a great bloc of voters [the unborn] who simply are not going to be taken in by the lopsided and distorted versions of the truth that are presented to the American public through the various media. (22)

The situation worsens when the Boy Scouts (of all people!) picket the White House, accusing the President of favoring sexual intercourse (of all things!)— *"between people,"* as the badly shaken Dixon puts it. The times are desperate, the need for a remedy clear. So (dressed in a football uniform) Dixon holds a "skull session" in his blast-proof underground locker room. One strategy involves a "secret operation for the surgical removal of the sweat glands" from Dixon's upper lip; another requires the sort of courage Dixon wrote about in SIX HUNDRED CRISES:

> ... if in order to accomplish those two important tasks
> I have to go on TV and say I am a homosexual, then
> I will do it. I had the courage to call Alger Hiss a
> Communist. I had the courage to call Khrushchev a
> bully. I assure you, I have the courage now to call
> myself a queer! (39)

But when he learns to his dismay that "homo-
sexuals have intercourse also" ("They do? . . . How?"
Dixon asks, stunned and then shocked when his "Spiritual Coach" provides a description), the plan is
scrubbed. After his "Military Coach" suggests that
they "get it over with once and for all. Shoot 'em!"
and his "Legal Coach" points out some of the potential
complications, they settle on a safer plan all around:
Pin the rap on somebody else.

As Roth imagines it, the list of possible fall guys
is insignificant compared with the actual White House
"enemies list"; his version includes fashionable rads
from the Berrigans to Jane Fonda. Nixon, of course,
widened the scope considerably and files on less spec-
tacular citizens compiled by the FBI, the CIA, and
other agencies are still being investigated as I write
these lines. In *Our Gang*, however, it is hardly surprising that Curt Flood (ex-baseball player, instigator
of a law suit against organized baseball, and recent de-
fector to Copenhagen) draws the short straw. He will
be the man made responsible for the conspiracy that
has turned the Boy Scouts of America into unwitting
dupes. In a world mad enough to think that way in the
first place, he is a "sensible" choice.

At this point *Our Gang* mushrooms consequences
until it looks as if Laurel and Hardy were its co-
authors. To be sure, more than some innocent pie
throwing is at stake. Dixon attacks Denmark and
"liberates" Elsinore, Hamlet's castle. The uncharitable

might interpret this act as aggression, even (God forbid!) imperialism! But that, in a word, would be "wrong." As Dixon explains in his famous "Something is Rotten in Denmark" speech:

> If, however, Copenhagen should refuse to negotiate in good faith by giving us what we want [Hamlet's castle], I shall immediately order 100,000 armed American troops onto Danish soil.
>
> Now, quickly, let me make one thing very clear: this will not constitute an invasion, either. Once we have overrun the country, bombarded the major cities, devastated the countryside, destroyed the military, disarmed the citizenry, jailed the leaders of the Pro-Pornography government, and established in Copenhagen the government currently in exile so that, as Abraham Lincoln said, it shall not perish from this earth, we shall immediately withdraw our troops.
>
> For unlike the Danes, this great country harbors no designs on foreign territory. (91–92)

Transposing the keys (for Denmark, read Vietnam, etc.) allows Roth the luxury of some escalations of his own; political obfuscation is raised to even wackier heights. It makes for a good, probably necessary, catharsis, but not the sort Aristotle had in mind.

Much of *Our Gang* is hopelessly dated even now: For instance, parodies about Spiro Agnew's fondness for the alliterative phrase (to the National Sword Swallowers Association, he says: "—the psychotics, the sob sisters, the skin merchants, the saboteurs, the self-styled Sapphos. . .") have become, as the jingoism would have it, "inoperative." And like the rest of us, Mr. Roth no longer has a Nixon to kick around.

Interestingly enough, some of my objections are answered in the grotesque way in which the book's original premise doubles back on itself, and a highly "poetic" justice seems to be served. Shortly after the

infamous Denmark speech, Dixon is not only assassi-
nated, but "bent into the fetal position, inside a large
transparent baggie, and tied shut at the top." Add a
mob bent on being arrested for the murder (citizens
queue up in long, unruly lines to make their "confessions"), and the comic bedlam is complete.

As for Dixon: he ends the book with a speech
from hell, on the comeback trail once more. This time,
however, his enemy is Righteousness ("For let there
be no mistake about it: . . . the God of Peace is out,
as He Himself has said, 'to crush' us 'under his feet.' ")
and all the familiar earmarks of a celestial conspiracy.
One suspects that in hell he has found the mandate
he has been searching for.

The Breast is a static novel, one even more severe-
ly limited by its controlling gimmick than *Our Gang*.
But this time the initial premise is literary rather than
political, and the result is comic allegory rather than
satirical invective. As the book jacket baldly declares:
"It is the story of the man who turned into a female
breast." For all of Portnoy's wild flights into grotesque
fantasy, there was enough about him that touched
common ground. In his case, the built-in constraints of
an analyst's couch struck readers as exactly the right
locale for a confession–complaint.

In *The Breast*, however, that necessary level of
particularity Roth had once insisted upon gives way
to a more symbolic "hoit." By this I mean to suggest
two things: first, that *The Breast*, like *Our Gang*, is
more "exercise" than novel, and, second, that its very
"symbolism" (whether taken comically, seriously or
on some ironic level in between) overwhelms more
mundane, but essential, elements like "story." Moreover, I am convinced that prolonged discussions about
The Breast as a contemporary reworking of Franz

Kafka's famous story "The Metamorphosis" or Nicolai Gogol's equally famous "The Nose" will not quite do. Surely Roth means to call our attention to them, but the recognition that he is sharing in a highbrow allusion is not quite the same thing as critically judging the work of art at hand. All puns aside, *The Breast* must support itself.

Besides, Roth had sounded echoes to Kafka earlier: In *Portnoy's Complaint*, for example, one of Alex's tirades includes the following:

> Say you're sorry, Alex. Say you're sorry! *Apologize!*[2]
> Yeah, for what? What have I done now? Hey, I'm
> hiding under my bed, my back to the wall, refusing to
> say I'm sorry, refusing, too, to come out and take the
> consequences. *Refusing*! And she is after me with a
> broom, trying to sweep my rotten carcass into the open.
> Why, shades of Gregor Samsa! Hello Alex, goodbye
> Franz! (121)

To be sure, Kafka's anguished, often unfinished and always puzzling fictions are a shorthand of modernity itself. His nightmares speak to an age growing accustomed to dark dreams, one burdened by bureaucracy and troubled with ill-defined guilts. In an intriguing essay entitled "Looking at Kafka," Roth broods over

---

2. Kafka is not the only literary echo; that Alex is urged to *"Apologize"* so traumatically reminds one of the opening pages of Joyce's *A Portrait of the Artist as a Young Man*:
    . . . He [Stephen Dedalus] hid under the table. His mother said:
            —O, Stephen will apologize.
            Dante said:
            —O, if not, the eagles will come and pull out his eyes.
        Pull out his eyes,
        Apologize,
        Apologize,
        Pull out his eyes.

a photograph of Kafka taken in 1924 (when Kafka was forty) and the coincidences that draw one man, uneasily, to another. At the time the essay was written, Roth was also forty. "Looking at Kafka" is a curious hybrid: not quite literary criticism, although Roth has a deep understanding of Kafka's life and art, and not quite an impressionist memoir about himself. Both elements are there, intertwined by a complex fate and each shedding light upon the other.

Roth focuses on the Kafka of 1924 because that was the crucial year he *"found himself transformed in his bed into a father, a writer, and a Jew."*[3] Philip Roth's latest book, *My Life as a Man,* is a bitter account of a similar (albeit, largely failed) transformation. Even more importantly, Roth turns to Kafka for a model of guilt metamorphosed into artful play, for sagas of "hoit" that can coexist with a comic vision. It was only when Roth realized that "this morbid preoccupation with punishment and guilt was all so funny" that a book like *Portnoy's Complaint* became possible.[4] And, if an author's own words can be believed, it was Kafka, more than any other writer who made the difference:

> I was strongly influenced in this book [*Portnoy's Complaint*] by a sit-down comic named Franz Kafka and the very funny bit he does called "The Metamorphosis." . . . there is certainly a personal element in the book, but not until I had got hold of guilt, you see, as a *comic idea,* did I begin to feel myself lifting free and clear of my last book, and my old concerns.

3. Philip Roth, "Looking at Kafka," *New American Review* #17 (New York: New American Library, 1973), 103.
4. Philip Roth, "Philip Roth's Exact Intent," interview with George Plimpton, *New York Times Book Review* (23 February 1959) 25.

In *The Breast*, Roth turns fabulator, giving his kinship with Kafka full comic rein. His contemporary version of Gregor Samsa's strange metamorphosis— Alan David Kepesh turning into a female breast rather than a beetle—translates the angst of one age into the self-conscious, stridently flip posture of another. The result is more an academic in-joke than a *roman à clef* as Kepesh, a professor of comparative literature, becomes the unwitting victim of too much "teaching," too intensely done. As Kepesh hypothesizes, what has happened to him

> ". . . might be my way of *being* a Kafka, being a Gogol, being a Swift. They could *envision* these marvelous transformations—they were artists. They had the language and those obsessive fictional brains. I didn't. So I had to live the thing."[5]

Roth has visited enough academic watering holes in the last few years (interestingly enough, "Looking at Kafka" was dedicated to his students at the University of Pennsylvania) to know the type well. If *The Breast* is, among other things, a highly ingenious way of biting the hands that have fed him, it is hardly an unusual phenomenon, given the new patronage universities provide. In any event, to Kepesh's list of impressive "theys," we must now, presumably, add the name of Philip Roth.

Granted, not all the jokes in *The Breast* are so unabashedly highbrow. There are moments when Kepesh's wit turns inward, when a capacity for black humor takes the edge off even *his* predicament:

5. Philip Roth, *The Breast* (New York: Holt, Rinehart and Winston, 1972), p. 72. (Hereafter page numbers appear in parentheses.)

81

I don't forsee a miracle. . . I suspect it's a little late
for that, and so it is not with such hope beating eternally
in the breast that the breast continues to want to
exist. (21)

And, too, there are the comic visits of Kepesh's
father, formerly the owner of a hotel in South Falls-
burg, New York, called the Hungarian Royale. Now
retired, he visits his son, apparently (or is it, perhaps,
resolutely?) oblivious to what has transpired:

> . . . seated in a chair that is drawn up close to my
> nipple, he recounts the current adventures of people who
> were our guests when I was a boy. Remember Abrams
> the milliner? Remember Cohen the chiropodist?
> Remember Rosenheim with the card tricks and the
> Cadillac? Yes, yes, yes, I think so. Well, this one is dying,
> this one has moved to California, this one has a son
> who married an Egyptian. (26)

All this while he, of course, has a son who turned into
a breast! But it is hard to sustain the evasive small-
talk (for Roth as well as Mr. Kepesh), even in a book
of less than eighty, wide-margined pages.

The real question in this book—Kafkaesque seriousness aside and bits of black humor to the contrary
—is "Why a breast?" Not since that idiotic exercise in
pornography called *Deep Throat* has anyone played
so fast and loose with human biology. Blaming it on
something called a "massive hormonal influx," Kepesh
is presumably converted

> . . . into a mammary gland disconnected from any human
> form, a mammary gland such as could only appear,
> one would have thought, in a dream or a Dali painting.
> They tell me that I am now an organism with the
> general shape of a football, or a dirigible. (12)

At one point Kepesh speculates about the possibility of it all being a "wish," one all too literally ful-

filled. Given Portnoy's breakdown and the psychiatric case studies to follow (Smitty in *The Great American Novel*; Peter Tarnopol in *My Life as a Man*), Kepesh, too, looks like a prime candidate for the looney bin. But he vigorously denies psychological explanations of his "breast"—and advises readers to resist them as well:

> No, the victim does not subscribe to the wish-fulfillment theory, and I advise you not to, neat and fashionable and delightfully punitive as it may be. Reality is grander than that. Reality has more style. There. For those of you who cannot live without one, a moral to this tale. "Reality has style," concludes the embittered professor who became a female breast. Go, you sleek, self-satisfied Houhynhnms, and moralize on that! (34)

If I am right about *The Breast*'s mode as one of comic allegory, it is "allegory" of a very playful, post-Modern, sort. To talk pedantically about, say, the breast fetish in American culture (see Woody Allen's delightful spoof in *Everything You Wanted to Know About Sex*) or about Kafkan themes in current fiction is to miss both the pain and the wit of Roth's novella.

What *The Breast* retains, however, is that strident voice generously sprinkled with exclamation points. Predictably enough, it cries out for more sex, more ingeniously performed. Not that Kepesh enjoys sex, for all his escalating demands and kinky tastes; like other Roth protagonists, he is grimmest in the bedroom. Moreover, as fashionable paradox would have it (for example, those considered "insane" are, often, saner than you or I), Kepesh insists that *he* is not the abnormal one. After all, in a world where a person can wake up as a female breast, what could make sense? Therefore, when Kepesh suggests that a prostitute

83

have sex with him (Claire, his ex-mistress is, it seems, too prudish), normal assumptions about the "grotesque" are up for grabs:

> Why shouldn't I have it [sex] if I want it! It's insane otherwise! I should be allowed to have it all day long! This is no longer ordinary life and I am not going to pretend that it is! *You* want me to be *ordinary—you* expect me to be *ordinary* in this condition! I'm supposed to be a sensible man—when I am like this! But that's crazy on your part, Doctor! . . . Why shouldn't I have anything and everything I can think of *every single minute of the day* if that can transport me from this miserable hell! . . . Instead I lie here being sensible! That's the madness, Doctor, *being sensible!* (36–37)

I suspect Roth has been itching to make such adolescent proclamations (italics and all) for some time. Instant gratifications—rather than normal operating procedures—are the only way one can respond to the mad world as it is. Given the political climate and/or the residues of societal repression, *Our Gang* and *The Breast* pass themselves off as "liberating" acts. But they are the product of writing fiction in a shoddy cultural moment, one which forgets that authentic freedom is more difficult to achieve, that even expressing the "hoit" requires deeper thought. Nonetheless, with these matters finally off his chest—*The Breast* removed as it were—Roth could begin to deal with the heart as well as the erogenous zones.

ON THE TRAIL, ONCE AGAIN, OF THE G.A.N.

IN a memorable moment from William Dean Howells' *A Hazard of New Fortunes* (1890), a gingerly, would-be writer wonders if he can put a character "into literature just as she was, with all her slang and brag"; he decides, alas, that he cannot and resigns himself to the view that "the great American novel, if true, must be incredible." Whatever faults Philip Roth might have as a writer, timidity is not one of them. *The Great American Novel* is full of "slang and brag." Half an attempt to give the whole notion of the G.A.N. (Great American Novel) the comic burial it deserves, half an attempt to write that "big book" his critics kept demanding, the results could only be disappointing. After all, Roth was only half joking about his title, and his readers were painfully aware of the oblique angle. As the epigraph from Frank Norris makes clear: ". . . the Great American Novel is not extinct like the Dodo, but mythical like the Hippogriff." Unfortunately, that very shrewd observation applies to Roth's novel as well.

But if *The Great American Novel* is not the G.A.N. writers and critics (particularly in the nineteenth century) had taken so seriously, it is, nonetheless, a genuinely comic look at our national literature as seen through the special prisms provided by our national pastime. Roth is thus working simultaneously in two great traditions: the one, that skeptical irony that characterized twentieth-century "answers" to the continuing demand for a G.A.N.; the other, that metaphorical use of baseball that provided a structure for such novels as Bernard Malamud's *The Natural* (1952), Robert Coover's *The Universal Baseball Association* (1969) or Barry Beckham's *Runner Mack* (1972).

A bit of literary history about the G.A.N. may be helpful: In 1929, for example, a charlatan named MacFadden launched a publication called "The Great American Magazine." The editors solicited nominations for the G.A.N. in an editorial policy that combined the democratic spirit with unabashed hucksterism:

> What is the greatest American novel you have ever read? . . . The Board of Editors of the MacFadden Publications will try to find each month a novel that will stir both the heart and the imagination. To do this, we must ask the help of our readers, who are the ultimate judge of what is best. This is an appeal to you, Every-reader! . . . Mention the reasons why you consider it a really great American novel, and, if you like, a few words about the influence this book has exercised on your life.[1]

The less said about their "nominations" the better, but it is clear that a writer like Philip Roth would not have been the inspirational choice in 1929, nor would *the* Philip Roth fare much better were a similar poll to be conducted tomorrow.

As serious writers grew skeptical about writing (or even reading) that elusive animal known as the G.A.N., satirical twists on the model became more probable. In 1938 Clyde Brion Davis published a book

1. Quoted in George Knox's "The Great American Novel: Final Chapter," *American Quarterly*, XXI (Winter 1969), 668, I am much indebted to not only this article, but to helpful conversations with Professor Knox about that baggy monster abbreviated as the G.A.N. For a detailed history of nineteenth-century attitudes, see his article "In Search of the Great Novel," *Western Review*, V (Summer 1968), 64–77.

entitled *"The Great American Novel,"* which spoofed
the earnestness with which young authors pursued the
goal of the G.A.N. His antiheroic protagonist is more
journalist than literary artist (he keeps a running account of his pathetic novel-in-progress) and more a
variation on the Horatio Alger mold than any serious
writer. But Davis's book was heavyhanded and generally unappreciated. Philip Roth, who did careful re-
search about baseball in the Hall of Fame Museum in
Cooperstown, New York, and read books like *Per-
centage Baseball*, probably did not encounter Davis's
"The Great American Novel" on some dusty library
shelf.

There were, of course, other overtly declared can-
didates for the honors: William Carlos Williams' *The
Great American Novel* and Gertude Stein's *The Making of Americans* come to mind as two of the most
serious and noteworthy attempts to forge an authentic
G.A.N. But that mixed bag of expectations and/or
illusions, American Dreams turned American Nightmares we associate with the Great American Novel
has moved, inevitably, toward the self-consciousness
of parody.[2] As Howells' character put it, with more
truth than he realized: ". . . the great American novel,
if true, must be incredible."

Contemporary American novelists have found a

2. As Hugh Kenner put it in an article on William Carlos
Williams' *The Great American Novel* entitled "A Note on 'The
Great American Novel,'" *Perspective*, VI (Autumn-Winter
1953), 177–82: "The lad who was going to produce 'The Great
American Novel' as soon as he had gotten his mind around
his adolescent experience is part of the folklore of the twenties,
and the prevalence of this myth documents the awareness of
the young American of thirty years ago that the consciousness
of his race remained uncreated." Now, of course, it is the
G.A.F. (Great American Film), rather than the G.A.N. that
receives such loving illusions from the sensitive young.

87

convenient metaphor for this necessary ingredient of the "incredible" in the *incredible* game of baseball. Roth's own fascination with the sport was foreshadowed early in eloquent descriptions by the usually hassled Alexander Portnoy:

> Thank God for center field! . . . Because center field is like some observations post, a kind of control tower, where you are able to see everything and everyone, to understand what's happening the instant it happens, not only by the sound of the struck bat, but by the spark of movement that goes through the infielders in the first second that the ball comes flying at them; and once it gets beyond them, "It's mine," you call, "it's mine," and then after it you go. For in center field, if you can get to it, it is yours. (68)

In *The Great American Novel*, however, such pastoral visions become paranoid fantasies. Rather than the turf of a center field over which a Portnoy can reign supreme, there is the sinking feeling in *The Great American Novel* that someone, or something, is controlling our lives. An omnipotent, but ill-defined, *they* emerge as the major force that moves contemporary society chaotically along. This, at least, is the view taken by the book's narrator, an eighty-seven-year-old ex-sports reporter named (of all things) Word Smith. As the writer of a now defunct column called "One Man's Opinion," it is his general opinion that evil forces have formed a conspiracy to change our nation's history, and his particular obsession is that they have singled out baseball's defunct Patriot League for special abuse. It is this tale of the Patriot League, told by a senile crusader, full of comic sound and fury, which comprises *The Great American Novel*. And like all stories of this stripe, it either signifies "nothing," or, perhaps, *everything*.

"Call me Smitty" the narrator remarks casually in the novel's opening line, thereby giving fair warning of even more outrageous literary parodies to come. The novel's "Prologue" bears an affinity not only to *Moby-Dick* (with its themes of alienation and outcasthood announced in its famous: "Call me Ishmael.") but also to literary "Prologues" from Chaucer's opening lines of *The Canterbury Tales* to the "Custom House" introduction of Hawthorne's *The Scarlet Letter*. Smitty, however, works on his particular novel-in-progress from a very different setting—the Valhalla Home for the Aged. Once again, Roth finds a congenial setting for his protagonist among the marginal, the infirm, or the mentally broken down.

Smitty is a man in his alliterative cups, the compiler of Rabelasian lists that run the comic gamut from one end of the alphabet to the other. A partial listing, for example, of those who "call him Smitty" include:

> . . . the boxers, the Brahmins, the brass hats, the British
> (*Sir* Smitty as of '36), the broads, the broadcasters,
> the broncobusters, the brunettes, the black bucks down
> in Barbados (*Meestah* Smitty), the Buddhist monks in
> Burma, one Bulkington, the bullfighters, the bullthrowers, the burlesque comics and burlesque stars, the bushmen, the bums, and the butlers. And that's only the
> letter B, fans, only *one* of the Big Twenty-Six![3]

As Smitty's doctor (psychiatrist?) suggests, this "orgy of alliteration . . . strikes me as wildly excessive and just a little desperate." Some of Roth's critics might agree with the diagnosis. Reviewing *The Great American Novel*, Marvin Mudrick took the occasion to chastise Roth and a number of our other well-known

3. Philip Roth, *The Great American Novel* (New York: Holt, Rinehart and Winston, 1973), p. 1. (Hereafter page numbers appear in parentheses.)

literary swingers who write "so-called comic novels [to] invent monsters merely as laboriously disagreeable as themselves."[4] Perhaps he is right, although I am more disturbed about those moments in *The Great American Novel* when Roth descends to that level of cute philosophizing that has made Kurt Vonnegut, Jr., such a cultish writer for the young:[5]

> Surprising, given the impact of the fart on the life of the American boy, how little you still hear about it; . . . On the other hand, that may be a blessing in disguise; this way at least no moneyman or politician has gotten it into his head yet to cash in on its nostalgic appeal. Because when that happens, you can kiss the fart goodbye. They will cheapen and degrade it until it is on a level with Mom's apple pie and our flag. Mark my words: as soon as some scoundrel discovers there is a profit to be made off of the American kids' love of the fart, they will be selling artificial farts in balloons at the circus. And you can just imagine what they'll smell like too. Like *everything* artificial. (13)

The bulk of *The Great American Novel*, however, is given over to Smitty's testy desire to have the truth about the Patriot League be known, to make them the mythological subject of his alliterative epic. When well-meaning ("sane") people suggest that he act his age, Smitty replies with that tough-minded, and self-righteous, stance that continues to be Roth's characteristic posture: ". . . what I want is for them to admit THE TRUTH!" In effect, Smitty constitutes a majority of one, a sentiment that puts him in very good Ameri-

4. Marvin Mudrick, "Old Pros with News from Nowhere," *Hudson Review*, XXVI:3 (Autumn 1973), 545.

5. In one of those intriguing coincidences that happen from time to time in contemporary literature, the latest fiction by both Roth and Vonnegut share a common fascination with a breakfast cereal called "Wheaties," as both product and imaginative possibility.

can company indeed. Each year at Cooperstown he continues to cast his ballot for Luke Gofannon (the greatest slugger in Patriot League history), but, alas, the conspiracy against him is so insidious that no Patriot League player is ever elected to the Hall of Fame, nor are Smitty's futile votes even recorded.

Smitty is, indeed, a "Word Smith" of the Old School: card-playing confidant and prose polisher to no less than *four* presidents (in an outrageous pun, even for Roth, one had claimed he would "rather be a writer than President"), he is a hard-boiled author in the hard-boiled Hemingway tradition. In fact, Hem (what Smitty called Hemingway—who, in turn, called *him* "Frederico") once pontificated as follows:

> "Frederico, you know the son of a bitch who is going to write The Great American Novel?"
> "No, Hem. Who?"
> "You." (24)

As Smitty (a.k.a. Frederico), Hemingway and a Vassar co-ed who had "come South to learn about Real Life" discuss "Literatoor," the shoptalk makes for comically easy pickings. When, for example, the Vassar girl claims that *Moby-Dick* was "about Good and Evil . . . the white whale was not just a white whale, it was a symbol," Hem erupts as only the hairy-chested can:

> "Vassar, *Moby-Dick* is a book about blubber, with a madman thrown in for excitement. Five hundred pages about blubber, one hundred pages of madman, and about twenty pages of how good niggers are with the harpoon." (27)

Later, even Poe's "Raven" has a swoop-on, one-liner as this zany hodge-podge of literary gossip allusion begins to develop a steam all its own:

> ". . . You know why you can't name the Great American
> Novel, Vassar?"
>
> "No," she moaned.
>
> "Because it hasn't been written yet! Because when it is
> it'll be Papa who writes it and not some rummy
> sportswriter. . ."
>
> Whereupon a large fierce gull swooped down,
> its broad wings fluttering, and opened its hungry beak
> to cry at Ernest Hemingway, "*Nevermore!*"
>
> "You can't quoth that to me and get away with
> it, you sea gull son of a bitch!" . . .
>
> Hem raced down to the cabin but when he returned
> with his pistol the gull was gone.
>
> "I ought to use it on myself," said Papa. "And if
> that bastard sea gull is right, I will." (30–31)

Smitty continues the literary pyrotechnics by re-
telling the American classics as if they were baseball
stories. Thus, *The Scarlet Letter* becomes R—"at the
outset R for Ruppert, the team's home; in the end, as
many would have it, for 'Rootless,' for 'Ridiculous,'
for 'Refugee' "; *The Adventures of Huckleberry Finn*
becomes the wacky story of how Nigger Jim and his
famous "hairball" grew, like Topsy, into Satchel Page
and his famous fastball; and *Moby-Dick* becomes the
archetypal allegory of American baseball itself:

> Who is Moby Dick if not the terrifying Ty Cobb of
> his species? Who is Captain Ahab if not the un-
> appeasable Dodger manager Durocher, or the steadfast
> Giant John McGraw? Who are Flask, Starbuck, and
> Stubb, Ahab's trio of first mates, if not the Tinker,
> Evers, and Chance of the *Pequod*'s crew? (41)

So much for Smitty's (and Roth's) parodic mode. *The
Great American Novel* is chock full of such academic
jokes, funny enough for those who get the "point,"
boring to them that don't.

After alliterating and alluding enough to "get the
waters running," Smitty settles down to the main busi-

ness at hand—namely, the tragicomic scenario of the Ruppert Mundys. Once a noble ballclub (in the days when superstars like Luke Gofannon, Base Ball, and Smoky Woden made the Mundys a household word),[6] they have degenerated into the sad sacks of organized baseball. When their owners, who have a quick eye for the fast buck, realize that Mundy Park can be turned into a wartime embarkation camp, they jump at the chance to combine patriotism with big profits. Homeless, the Ruppert Mundys must play their entire schedule on the road, and as if to add insult to injury, the perpetual "visitors" find themselves paraded through the opposition's street in garbage trucks.

The treatment is as cruel as it is appropriate. They are, after all, a ragged lot: The Mundys boast a one-legged catcher, a one-armed pitcher, an outfielder with a penchant for running into walls, and a group Smitty describes ruefully as "the has-beens, might-have-beens, should-have-beens, would-have-beens, never-weres and never-will-bes." There is even a four-teen-year-old who desperately wants that essential of big-league ballplayers, a nickname all his own:

> "How about Hank?" he asked his new teammates his very first day in the scarlet and white, "don't I look like a Hank to you guys?" He was so green they had to sit him down and *explain* to him that Hank was a nickname for Henry. "Is that your name, boy—Henry?" Nope. It's worse . . . Hey, how about Dutch? Dutch Damur. It rhymes!" "Dutch is for Dutchman, knucklehead." "Chief?" "For Injuns." "Whitey?" "For blondes." (100)

In the end he is called (what else?) Nickname Damur.

But the saga of the hapless Mundys is only half

6. Like most of the names in *The Great American Novel*, these have both mythic resonances and comic configurations. At least part of Roth's parodic scheme is to push literary pre-tentiousness into that corner known as excess.

the story; the other side of *The Great American Novel* is fashioned from heroic stuff. That is, Roth widens the possibilities of slapstick humor by incorporating those mythological elements usually reserved for more "serious" fiction. In Malamud's *The Natural,* for example, the mythopoeic life of Roy Hobbes is built upon a carefully diagramed substructure drawn from T. S. Eliot's *The Waste Land,* Frazer's *Golden Bough,* and the best that academic critics have thought and said. In the fifties such exercises seemed more impressive than they do some twenty years later. By more recent standards Malamud strains too much, and as a result, his novel is fraught with the creaking of archetypal gears. Roth, on the other hand, plays his mythic cards with a light touch. Luke Gofannon, whose career is similar to Babe Ruth's in more than a few aspects, dies the death of a hero, albeit one with black humor heavily shaded in:

> The legislature of the state, in special session, voted him New Jersey license plate 372 in commemoration of his lifetime batting average. People would look for that license plate coming along the road down there in Jersey, and they'd just applaud when it came by. And Luke would tip his hat. And that's how he died that winter. To acknowledge the cheers from an on-coming school bus—boys and girls hanging from every window, screaming, "It's him! It's Luke!"—the sweetest, shyest ballplayer who ever hit a homer, momentarily took his famous hands from the wheel and his famous eyes from the road, and shot off the slick highway into the Raritan River. (84)

Even more bizarre is the story of the most fabulous pitcher in Patriot League history, Gil Gamesh. In the Babylonian epic of the same name, he is a hero of Herculean proportions; in America, however, Gil's heritage is reduced to an ethnic "Bab" joke:

And so that's what I wrote down in school too, under
what I was: Babylonian. And that's how come they
started throwin' rocks at me. . . . they'd all take turns
chasin' me home from school. First for a few blocks the
Irish kids threw rocks at me. Then the German kids
threw rocks at me. Then the Eye-talian, then the
colored . . .—hell, even the Jew kids threw rocks at
me, while they was runnin' away from the kids throwin'
rocks at them. . . . "Get outta here, ya' lousy little
Babylonian bastard! Go back to where you belong,
ya' dirty bab!" (254)

In revenge, Gil Gamesh becomes a pitcher, first
with rocks against hostile bigots and then with base-
balls against opposing hitters. As a nineteen-year-old
rookie, he threw an astounding six consecutive shut-
outs in his first six starts. He was, in short, virtually
unhittable, that is, until he ran into an umpire named
Mike "the Mouth" Masterson. Their feud reaches its
tragic climax when Mike inadvertently turns his back
on the final pitch of the most perfectly pitched game
ever recorded[7] (Gamesh had retired twenty-six batters
on seventy-eight consecutive strikes and there was a
2–0 count on the remaining batter). Enraged, Gil
throws a rising fastball that hits Mike "the Mouth" in
(where else?) the mouth and reduces him, instantly,
to a mute. For the "good of the game," Gil Gamesh is
forever banished from organized baseball.

Later, his car is found demolished near Bingham-
ton, New York, and Gil Gamesh is presumed dead.
But like the mythopoeic hero whose name he bears,

7. Mike later claims that he saw the kidnapper–
murderer of his daughter in the stands. Back in 1938 (his first
year up in the Patriot League) there had been a threat on his
daughter's life so he would make sure the Rustlers won. He,
of course, refuses to be intimidated, the Rustlers lose and "in
subsequent weeks, pieces of little Mary Jane Masterson were
found in every ball park in the Patriot League."

rumors about his stubborn immortality persist. He is reported as "riding the rails in Indiana, selling apples in Oklahoma City, or waiting in a soup line in L.A." Graffiti writers etch "I'LL BE BACK, G.G." on restroom walls. The handwriting is clear; a Gil Gamesh can never really die. Ordinary mortals always deny their heroes a grave.

Gil Gamesh is, of course, in excellent mythological company. Among the other names Roth includes for his lineup are Astarte, Baal, Demeter, and a pantheon of lesser gods. However, with the Mundys' long-suffering manager, Ulysses S. Fairsmith, Roth adds a dash of Christian martyrdom to the religious fabric that is already prevalent in the story. Fairsmith is a firm believer in the principle that "through suffering . . . they shall find their purpose and their strength." When the Mundys are sent into ignominious exile, he is ecstatic. Half a Moses, half a Christ, it is Fairsmith who insists that "Baseball is this country's religion" and that the Commissioner "let my players go."

Fairsmith also fancies himself as something of a missionary, one who can bring baseball to the savages. In an extended parody of Conrad's "The Heart of Darkness" (the funniest since the days of Saul Bellow's *Henderson the Rain King*), the natives take their comic revenge. They insist, it seems, on sliding into first base, even when walked! When Fairsmith objects (proper form is, after all, PROPER FORM), the savages strike back with an etiquette of their own. The result is an orgy of the imagination, one filled with a darker comedy than even Conrads "unspeakable rites" could contain: Virgins are ceremoniously defiled by baseball bats, leather gloves are boiled and eaten, shrunken heads used in batting practice, etc. Suspended from a pole, Fairsmith watches the desecration and says—as if on cue—"The horror! The horror!"

And, finally, there is Roland Agni (before Roland, place "Childe"; for Agni, read "Agonistes"). He has all the necessary equipment to be a superstar (his body "tapering like the V for victory from his broad shoulders . . . down to ankles as elegantly turned as Betty Grable's"), but, according to his worried parents, he lacks character:

> The boy had been hearing applause in his ears ever since he had hurled a perfect sandlot game at age six, with the result that over the years he had become, in his father's opinion, contemptuous of everything and everyone around him, above all of his family and the values of humility and self-sacrifice that they had tried, in vain, to instill in him. (122)

Becoming a Ruppert Mundy should take care of that! Unfortunately, Agni's Mundyhood only aggravates the situation. Because the pathetic Mundys are an endless source of frustration, he fiercely wants to be traded, and the story leads directly to those "temptations" usually associated with a Grail Knight. At one point he begs Angela Trust (her name is hardly accidental) to save him. As the owner of the Tri-City team and an ex-nymphomaniac turned right-wing fanatic, she had given aid and comfort to the likes of Babe Ruth, Luke Gofannon, and others who swung a big bat. Later, Agni even dabbles in a miracle product called "Jewish Wheaties," one that makes temporary winners of the Mundys and a pile of *gelt* for its young inventor, Isaac Ellis.

Roth is at his stylistic best as an anecdotal writer. That is, in short bursts, blackout, skits, hillarious asides, rather than in sustained, well-plotted narrative. *The Great American Novel* was probably as much fun to write as it is to read. Every conceivable "joke" about baseball, every possible comic inversion and allusion has been wrinkled in somewhere. However, such novels have the nasty habit of toppling over from too many comic building blocks, and something like that happens in *The Great American Novel*; it is a risk that comes with the territory. Like *Portnoy's Complaint*, exhaustion take its toll: one, literally, gets tired laughing.

There is, for example, the subplot that eventually pits a midget pitcher (O.K. Ockatur) against a midget pinch-hitter (Bob Yamm). The chapter is entitled, predictably enough, "Every Inch a Man." The story begins when Frank Mazuma, the Kakoola owner as interested in money as his name suggests, signs Yamm as a pinch-hitter. Granted, we have been shown that tack before. What Roth does, however, is build on the comic possibilities not explored in "It Happens Every Spring." Midget jokes explode everywhere: On a radio show, for example, Mrs. Yamm is asked if "there are any little Yamms at home" and

> . . . a famous illustrator of the era penned a tribute to Yamm on the cover of *Liberty* magazine that was subsequently reprinted by the thousands and came to take its place on the walls of just about every barber shop in America in those war years—the meticuously realistic drawing entitled "The Midgets' Midget," showing Bob in his baseball togs, his famous fraction on his back [¼], waving his little bat toward an immense cornucopia decorated with forty-eight stars; marching out of the cornucopia are an endless stream of what appears to be leprechauns and elves from all walks of life: tiny little doctors with stethoscopes, little nurses, little factory workers in overalls, little tiny professors wearing glasses and carrying little books under their arms . . . (192)

In the best Norman Rockwell fashion, America takes this straight-arrow midget to its collective heart. O.K. Ockatur, however, wants no part of this chauvinistic, sentimental slop. He is a midget libber, and an embittered one to boot. The eventual showdown on the diamond between Yamm and Ockatur is as well paced as it is hysterical.

The same effect results from the grotesque game between the inept Mundys and a pick-up team from a mental asylum. Roth pulls out all the stops: a catatonic fielder who goes into trances, an exhibitionist catcher who flashes obscene signals, and a kleptomaniac baserunner who finally steals the ball. When the Mundys celebrate their "victory," only Roland Agni seems able to realize that *They were madmen! They were low as low can be!* But it is hard to tell the "professionals" from the patients without a program. Where else could a Ruppert Mundy like Specs Skirnir incur such comic injuries while sitting on the bench?

> Look, look how I chipped my tooth on the water
> fountain in Independence. My glasses got steamed up on
> account of the heat, and I went in too close for a drink,
> and I chipped my tooth on the spout. . . . Look, Cholly,
> look at my shins, they're all black and blue—tripped
> over Big Jawn's foot just going down to the clubhouse
> in Terra Inc. to take a leak. Imagine—just taking a leak
> is dangerous in these damn things. . . . Nine innings just
> on the bench and at the end of the game I'm a
> wreck! (215)

Contemporary literature is filled with beautiful losers and sensitive flops. They provide, among other things, a temporary relief from our competitive society and an index of easy and nonthreatening identification. Still, the Ruppert Mundys may yet go down as the consummate "losers" of them all.

In *The Great American Novel* satire runs rampant from the Negro Patriot League—with teams like the Kakoola Boll Weevils or the Ruppert Rastuses, all owned by a tough-minded Aunt Jemima—to Ellis, the immigrant Jewish owner of the Greenbacks. While the former presents such comedy duos as "Teeth 'n Eyes" to amuse the crowd, the latter brings a bit of the Lower East Side to the grey pin stripes, sweat sox, and cleats:

> Reluctantly, the boy changed out of his threadbare church suit and his frayed white shirt into a fresh Greenback home uniform. "Nice," Ellis said, smiling, "*very* nice."
>
> "Ain't the seat kind a' baggy?"
>
> "The seat I can take in."
>
> "And the waist—"
>
> "De vaist I can fix, please. I'm talkin' general appearance. Sarah," he called, "come look at de new second-baseman."
>
> ". . . She'll pin de seat and de vaist, and you'll pick up *Vens*day."
>
> "*Wednesday*? What about tomorrow?"
>
> "Please, she already got t'ree rookies came in yesterday. Vensday! Now, how about a nice pair of spikes?" (266)

Like Joseph Heller's *Catch–22*, *The Great American Novel* is a difficult novel to resolve successfully. In both cases, the zany proves fatally attractive and contributes to the most arbitrary of endings. The last eighty pages of Roth's novel re-introduce the errant Gil Gamesh (now a repentent, ex-Russian spy) and that Communist plot Angela Trust had so feared. The novel's last section includes a quick succession of death rattles (assassinations, suicides, airplane crashes) and subsequent investigations by a witch-hunting Senate committee into the notorious "Mundy Thirteen." Word Smith is held in contempt (a poetic justice, indeed, for a writer of his ilk) and sentenced to a year in the Federal penitentiary. If Roth cannot quite put all the pieces of his plot into place, he, at least, manages to scatter them around.

Smitty alone is left to tell the sad tale of the now-expunged Patriot League: like the Ancient Mariner, like the mock Ishmael of his opening sentence. But the "Epilogue" suggests that rejection slips will be his unhappy lot. Nobody believes his story—or that he is sane for that matter. No doubt some of Roth's more plodding critics will see *The Great American Novel* as a study in illusion–reality, part of his ongoing effort to separate genuine vision from mere paranoia, truth from the official lie our society tells. But I prefer the words written to Smitty by an editor who may well have in mind some of Roth's own reservations about the book:

> Dear Mr. Smith,
>   I am returning your manuscript. Several people here found portions of it entertaining, but by and large the book seemed to most of us to strain for its effects and to simplify for the sake of facile satiric comment the complex realities of American political and cultural life. (378)

PETER TARNOPOL AND THE "HOITS" OF MANHOOD

IN *The Great American Novel* Roth carefully distanced himself from Smitty's obsessions and the chaotic forces that energized his novel-in-progress about the Patriot League. The pieties associated with the G.A.N., as well as American mythologies real and/or imagined, were given a comic burial in artifice. That is, Roth's literary self-consciousness kept the "hoit" at more than an arm's length. Smitty's saga may be edged with pain, but Roth's novel turns it into a wildly parodic romp. *My Life as a Man* (1974) reverses the process: Art turns into the Frankenstein monster, stalking Tarnapol with the banal, albeit painful, realities he so disastrously courted.

As I suggested earlier, *My Life as a Man* also completes that informal trilogy that gives Roth's canon the illusion of a seamless whole. Seen through Joycean prisms, it could be described this way: *Goodbye, Columbus* is *Dubliners* writ small, *Portnoy's Complaint*, a pale shadow of *A Portrait of the Artist as a Young Man* and *My Life as a Man*, a failed *Ulysses*. I mention the parallels not to play Joyce's trump against Roth's weak suit, but because it is a shorthand way of highlighting two radically different responses to the interactions between life and art.

In somewhat the spirit with which Leslie Fiedler, only half-joking, muses about writing a book entitled *What Was Literature?*, Peter Tarnopol, the edgy protagonist of *My Life as a Man*, shores up the ruins of his life against the "big book" he cannot quite imagine. He has been *had* by capital-L Literature. When in the fifties the noble subject of discussion was "responsibility," and literary criticism was full of solemn pronouncements about "the human tragedy," poor Tarnopol listened, read Thomas Mann et al., and dreamed of writing such fictions himself.

My Life as a Man is Tarnopol's turn at last. But as he confesses, "all I can do with my story is tell it. And tell it. And tell it. And that's the *truth*." If his sprawling autobiographical narrative keeps grating against the decorum of high art, what he calls "Useful Fictions"—two short stories about the adolescence and subsequent marriage of his alter ego Nathan Zuckerman—set the stage for Tarnopol's brooding. In effect, Roth adds yet another refracting mirror to the technique he had pioneered in *Portnoy's Complaint*. The gripes of Roth (this time, more adult and considerably more agonizing) are collapsed into a fictional persona who, in turn, collapses them still further into the object of his interior fiction.

The result are those literary Chinese boxes we identify as the reflexive mode. For earlier Modernists like Conrad and Gide, reflexivity meant not only that the activity of "storytelling" turned inward and against itself (for example, Marlow's difficulty as narrator articulating the story of Marlow-as-participant in "Heart of Darkness") but that "fiction" per se became a running account of its own creation. In Gide's *The Counterfeiters*, for example, a protagonist writing a novel keeps a journal about a novelist who also keeps a journal. The possibilities are as endless as they are dizzying—as Philip Quarles, the protagonist of Huxley's *Point Counter Point*, suggests in a ringing manifesto for this aspect of Modernism:

> Put a novelist into the novel. He justifies aesthetic generalizations, which may be interesting—at least to me. He also justifies experiment. Specimens of his work may illustrate other possible or impossible ways of telling a story. And if you have him telling parts of the same story as you are, you can make a variation on the theme. But why draw the line at one novelist inside your novel? Why not a second inside his? And a third inside the novel of the second? And so on to infinity, like those advertisements of Quaker Oats where there's a Quaker holding a box of oats, on which is a

picture of another Quaker holding another box of
oats, on which etc., etc. . . .

To this now-standard formula, Roth adds some
distinctly post-Modernist touches. Tarnopol's Zuckerman stories are followed by an avalanche of critical
opinion—from the editors of *Bridges'* magazine ("I
see in Zuckerman's devotion to Lydia . . . a kind of
allegory of Tarnopol and his Muse."), his sister, his
analyst, and, of course, himself. At one point Tarnopol
even speculates about his possible reactions when the
"truth," at last, is out:

> How will I like reading reviews of my private life in
> the Toledo *Blade* and the Sacramento *Bee*? And what will
> *Commentary* make of this confession? I can't imagine
> it's good for the Jews. What about when the professional
> marital experts and authorities on love settle in for
> a marathon discussion of my personality problems on
> the "David Susskind Show"?[1]

To be sure, Roth has no monopoly on such contemporary gamesmanship. In Joyce Carol Oates's *Expensive People*, Richard Everett includes full-length
(and wickedly delightful parodies they are!) reviews
of his novel-in-progress (entitled—what else?—*Expensive People*) in the *New York Times, Time*, the *New
Republic*, etc. And by way of confusing Art and Life
still further, he provides a psychological analysis of a
story by his mother (one fully reprinted in the text of
his "novel"), which had appeared in *The Quarterly
Review of Literature*—where, in fact, that story ("The
Molesters") had been published a few years earlier by
Miss Oates. John Barth—an artful dodger of long
standing—slips in and out of *Chimera* to make au-

1. Philip Roth, *My Life as a Man* (New York: Holt, Rinehart and Winston, 1974), p. 230. (Hereafter page numbers appear in parentheses.)

thorial comment about mythological heroes and his own work. Or one recalls Borges, writing fictitious (?) commentaries about fictitious (?) books or Nabokov, providing hilariously pedantic footnotes for an epical poem called *Pale Fire* or Donald Barthelme or any number of others.

But however much others may have raised the respectability of self-conscious fictionizing, I think Roth uses the technique for a radically different purpose in *My Life as a Man*. Tarnopol's problem is not merely a "writing block"; rather, it is the growing realization that *all* fiction (including his own and, perhaps, even Philip Roth's) has been a necessary falsification. If *Portnoy's Complaint* was an attempt to break through guilt into comic celebration, *My Life as a Man* is an effort to move beyond the constraints of literary Modernism, to confront "hoits" that have no pattern, no tragic resolution.

"Salad Days," the first of Tarnopol's "Useful Fictions," begins with a warning from Zuckerman's father as telling about Roth's early fiction as it is prophetic about Zuckerman: "Keep up that cockiness with people, Natie, and you'll wind up a hermit, a hated person, the enemy of the world." Moreover, "Salad Days" deepens that sense in which Alexander Portnoy played at being the sensitive young man at odds with family, religion, and state. To be sure, more than the names have been changed to protect the innocent; Zuckerman's childhood recollections are pastoral rather than traumatic, filled with securities rather than castrations:

> Twice his father had gone bankrupt in the years between the wars: Mr. Z.'s men's wear in the late twenties, Mr. Z.'s kiddies' wear in the early thirties; and yet never had a child of Z.'s gone without three

nourishing meals a day, or without prompt medical attention, or decent clothes, or a clean bed, or a few pennies "allowance" in his pocket. (5)

But annoyances do accompany such territory. The Zuckermans are hopelessly middle class, and Nathan labors mightily to cultivate that dispassion he equates with high-brow refinement. He must honor an undergraduate commitment to Thomas Wolfe's *Of Time and the River*, a theatrically high cost—in this case, depledging his fraternity. When his father asks if he has "got for a son all of a sudden— a *quitter*?" Nathan replies with an icy blend of moral righteousness and romantic posturing:

> "It's beneath my dignity, yes, that's correct" Or: "No,
> I'm not against things to be against them, I am against
> them on matters of principle." "In other words," said—
> seethed—Mr. Zuckerman, "you are right, if I'm getting
> the idea, and the rest of the world is wrong. Is that it,
> Nathan, you are the new god around here, and the
> rest of the world can just go to hell!" Coolly, coolly, so
> coolly that the most sensitive seismograph hooked into
> their long-distance connection would not have recorded
> the tiniest quaver in his voice: "Dad, you so broaden
> the terms of our discussion with a statement like
> that—" and so, temperate, logical, eminently "reason-
> able," just what it took to bring on the volcano in
> New Jersey. (13–14)

Neil Klugman remained convinced that these were the proper responses to heap upon philistines like Aunt Gladys and the Patimkins. Writing "Zuckerman's" memoirs, Tarnopol is less sure. In something of the same spirit with which James Wright ends one of his starkly confessional poems with the line: "I have wasted my life," Tarnopol sets out to etch his particulars in excruciating detail. Thus, while "Salad Days" maximizes the innocence and naivete associated

with the pretentious life of a pretentious student major-
ing in English, it also adds a dimension of remorse
missing in Roth's earlier work. Moreover, the voice
that speaks so candidly about regret is linked inextricably to one that whispers the unthinkable: Perhaps, just perhaps, they were right after all. I, too, have
wasted my life.

The psychic split I am suggesting is foreshadowed
in the two very different women who dominate the
parochial canvas of "Salad Days"—Miss Caroline Benson symbolizing the spirit and Sharon Shatzky, the
literally throbbing flesh. The pipe-puffing dean at Bass
College may insist that "the ivy on the library walls . . .
could be heard on certain moonlit nights to whisper the
word 'tradition,' " but Miss Benson hears only the
echoes of Bloomsbury. Zuckerman, of course, prefers
to follow his English teacher–surrogate parent into that
magical world where one pronounces the g in "length"
and aspirates the h in "whale," where one talks intensely about the moral landscape of *Pride and Preju-
dice* and where, if Chosen, he could take tea and water-
cress sandwiches in Miss Benson's "English" garden.

To be sure, there were other bright "New York
Jews" before Zuckerman and there would, no doubt,
be others to follow, but for the moment, it is Nathan
Zuckerman (formerly of Camden and the Mr. Z. shoe
store) who reads his senior thesis on "Subdued Hys-
teria: A Study of the Undercurrent of Agony in Some
Novels of Virginia Woolf" to an admiring (albeit, ultimately condescending) mentor:

> The paper was replete with all those words that now
> held such fascination for him, but which he had hardly,
> if ever, uttered back in the living room in Camden:
> "irony" and "values" and "fate," "will" and "vision"
> and "authenticity," and, of course, "human," for which

he had a particular addiction. . . . Suffering and failure, the theme of so many of the novels that "moved" him, were "human conditions" about which he could speak with an astonishing lucidity and even gravity by the time he was a senior honors student—astonishing in that he was, after all, someone whose own sufferings had by and large been confined up till then to the dentist's chair. (17)

On the other hand, Sharon Shatzky (daughter of Al "the Zipper King") is an X-rated version of Brenda Patimkin. If "Goodbye, Columbus" was shocking in the fifties, two decades of Pop Porn have forced Roth to raise the ante. To be—or not to be—the defiant owner of a diaphram is no longer a controversial question. Rather, Sharon concentrates on the kinkier possibilities often overlooked in, say, a zucchini. In this sense, Sharon's nonstop, breathtaking sexuality resembles that of the Monkey. And like the ambivalent Portnoy, Zuckerman finds the raw enthusiasm somewhat unsettling: "If Sharon had a fault as a student of carnality, it was a tendency to try a little too hard, with the result that her prose (to which Zuckerman, trained by Miss Benson in her brand of the New Criticism, was particularly attuned) often offended him by a too facile hyperbole."

One can safely assume that life will provide this "principled" young man with all the suffering for which he has developed such an exquisite taste. But being life—rather than art—the pain will seem even stranger and more contradictory than writing themes about the "human condition" had been. It will also "hoit" more deeply. In "Courting Disaster," the gap between what Zuckerman imagines as "serious" and what actually constitutes the quotidian reality grows wider. He is an older, though hardly wiser, version of the protagonist in the first of Tarnopol's "Useful Fictions." This time, however, some of the background information is altered: Zuckerman's father is a book-keeper, the maker of arithmetical puzzles called "Marking Down" and the one-time bohemian brother of "Salad Days" is replaced by a sister who listens to *Jerry Vale Sings Italian Hits* with her Italian husband and buys pink "harem" pillows for their summer house in the Italian Catskills. Zuckerman's "complaint," however, remains much the same:

> I could not easily make peace with the fact that I had a sister in the suburbs, whose pastimes and adornments —vulgar to a snobbish college sophomore, an elitist already reading Allen Tate on the sublime and Dr. Leavis on Matthew Arnold with his breakfast cereal— more or less resembled those millions upon millions of American families. (40)

"Courting Disaster" begins with that unbounded confidence only possible when budding esthetes divide the world into those sheltered beneath the groves of academe and the great unwashed who labor outside. Zuckerman is Stephen Dedalus's "priest of the imagination" with an elaborate syllabus and a tweed sports coat, the instructor of freshman composition waging holy wars against commas splices everywhere. Eisenhower, Norman Vincent Peale, *Time,* and General Motors all wither in the face of his mimeographed attacks and uncompromising classroom standards. Dedicated to his own talent, especially its boundless potential, Zuckerman is equally committed to his students and the converts to art they might, one day, become. In short, his is an orderly life, where ecstasy is stumbling across a slightly soiled copy of Empson's *Seven Types of Ambiguity* (although Zuckerman's own life had not even one!) or writing yet another "skillful impersonation of the sort of stories I had been taught to admire most in college—stories of 'The Garden Party' variety." Given enough time, one could predict the books on his shelf, the publications in his vita, and the comments scribbled across the papers from his freshman students.

> Reading—and noting—fifty pages a night, I could average three books a month, or thirty-six a year. I also knew approximately how many short stories I might expect to complete in a year, if I put in thirty hours at it a week; and approximately how many students' essays I could mark in an hour; and how large my "library" would be in a decade, if I were to continue to be able to make purchases in accordance with my present budget. (50)

Lydia Jorgenson Ketterer not only signals an end to this genteel, academically patterned life, but she reduces Zuckerman's heady metaphors to the level of soap opera melodrama. Initially, she is his student— one of the desperate adults in his night-school "creative writing" class—but soon it is Ketterer who provides a fatally attractive manifesto all her own. Zuckerman's first lecture, as ponderous as it is inappropriate, sets the tone of disasters to follow. For two hours he hectors the class with the best that Aristotle, James, Conrad, Flaubert, Joyce have thought and said about aesthetics. The air is filled with quotations from *Crime and Punishment, Anna Karenina, Madame Bovary,* and a host of other monuments with foreboding resonances. From Flaubert, for example, Zuckerman chooses a sentiment with more significance than he realized on that fateful night in 1957: "What seems to me the highest and most difficult achievement of Art is not to make us laugh or cry, or to rouse our lust or our anger, but to do as nature does—that is, fill us with wonderment."

110

Lydia supplies "wonderment" with a vengeance. Raped by her father and brutalized by the world in general, she has, somehow, managed not only to survive, but to have been "deepened by all that misery." Zuckerman, on the other hand, learned about suffering vicariously, by underlining the classic texts of the Great Tradition and keeping index cards about the footnotes. Lydia earned *her* unacknowledged Ph.D. in the subject first-hand. Moreover, she possesses a wisdom about herself that proves fatally attractive to the pampered boy from Camden.

To be sure, this situation has become a commonplace in American-Jewish literature. Zuckerman's brother Morris, a man with a talent for getting to the "bottom line" quickly, puts it this way:

> What is it with you Jewish writers? Madeleine Herzog, Deborah Rojack, the cutie-pie castrator in *After the Fall,* and isn't the desirable shiksa of *A New Life* a kvetch and titless in the bargain? And now, for the further delight of the rabbis and the reading public, Lydia Zuckerman, that Gentile tomato. Chicken soup in every pot, and a Grushenka in every garage. With all the Dark Ladies to choose from, you luftmenschen can really pick 'em.

To his list, I would add Stella, the prostitute–redeemer of Bernard Malamud's "The Magic Barrel"—less as an "influence" (a contention both Roth and Malamud would vigorously deny) than as two variations on a central theme. In Malamud's story, Leo Finkle is a rabbinical student who resorts to the services of a marriage broker when it becomes clear that (a) a wife would greatly enhance his chances for obtaining a congregation and (b) "apart from his parents, he had never loved anyone." Index card after index card is paraded before him, as if the shy Finkle were buying, say, a used car. With mounting anguish, Finkle rejects them all—all except a noncandidate who turns out to be, ironically enough, the marriage broker's daughter. Malamud describes Finkle's self-styled program for their mutual salvation:

> Her face deeply moved him. . . . It gave him the impression of youth—spring flowers, yet age—a sense of having been used to the bone, wasted. . . . It was not, he affirmed, that she had an extraordinary beauty— no, though her face was attractive enough; it was that *something* about her moved him . . . she—had *lived*, or wanted to—more than just wanted, perhaps regretted how she had lived—had somehow deeply suffered. . . . Though he prayed to be rid of her, his prayers went unanswered. Through days of torment he endlessly struggled not to love her; fearing success, he escaped it. He then concluded to convert her to goodness, himself to God. The idea alternately nauseated and exalted him.

And here is Roth on Zuckerman's fascination with Lydia:

> I was drawn to Lydia . . . because she had suffered so and because she was so brave. Not only that she had survived, but *what* she had survived, gave her enormous moral stature, or glamor, in my eyes: on the one hand, the puritan austerity, the prudery, the bland- ness, the xenophobia of the women of her clan; on the other, the criminality of the men . . . But where she was dry, brownish, weatherworn, I pressed my open mouth. I took no pleasure in the act, she gave no sign that she did; but at least I had done what I had been frightened of doing, put my tongue to where she had been brutalized, as though—it was tempting to put it this way—that would redeem us both. (70)

The similarities are obvious enough, even if one dis- counts some of them to critical selectivity. What in- terests me, however, are the curious differences. To be sure, "The Magic Barrel" is a short story, one that is allowed to end in a morally ambiguous tableau. We can, of course, speculate about the relationship between Rabbi Finkle and Stella, but we do not see them the next morning, the next month, the next year—a characteristic that is the province of a novel. Zuckerman's story begins, in effect, where Malamud's leaves off. Moreover, Malamud limits his vision to equations that link suffering with a poetically defined Jewishness. As his formula would have it: One discovers an essential humanity, regardless of the particulars involved, when one confronts the essential fact that "All men are Jews." So be it in the world of *The Assistant*, although I remain convinced that if the horrors of the twentieth century have taught us anything, it is that all men are *not* Jews.

By contrast, what Roth tests are the consequences of imposing literary metaphors onto the texture of lives at once more fixated and more sprawling than "fiction" proper can be. In *Portnoy's Complaint* masturbation was not only a matter of content, but also of form, the very rhythms of the novel seeming to derive from Portnoy's guilt-ridden "whacking off." In *My Life as a Man*, Zuckerman's grimly earnest act of cunnilingus leads to the sort of literary speculation that is always a prominent feature in novels about a protagonist's "failure" to produce his big book:

> *As though that* [cunnilingus] *would redeem us both*. A notion as inflated as it was shallow, growing, I am certain, out of "serious literary studies." Where Emma Bovary had read too many romances of her period, it would seem that I had read too much of the criticism of mine. . . . I could have done a clever job on myself for my senior honors thesis in college: "Christian Temptations in a Jewish Life: A Study in the Ironies of 'Courting Disaster.'" (72)

Considered historically, American-Jewish fiction seems always to be written in the confessional mode—in an ongoing assessment of the gains and losses that occur when religious impulses are secularized, when an ethnic fabric is acculturated. The result is a peculiar tension between the noise of a majority culture and that still, small voice we continue to recognize in our most important American-Jewish writers. For earlier American-Jewish writers the battle lines were drawn between the demands of Orthodoxy and the attractions of secular culture. Liberation from the parochial was achieved by a rigorous dedication to the likes of Flaubert and Joyce on one front and a nearly equal commitment to academia on the other. Writing in the fifties, Roth inherited the spoils of such "victories" and, at the same time, made enough waves, via *Goodbye, Columbus*, to make his own credentials as a rebel appear legitimate.

A decade and a half later, Roth would still find himself hard pressed to move beyond Modernism and the dues he kept paying (consciously or otherwise) to "great books." *Portnoy's Complaint* was, to be sure, a partial breakthrough, but a disintegrating marriage reeks more "hoit" than the most castrating mother can inflict upon the most smothered of Jewish sons. As Zuckerman discovers as he tries in vain to bring the "traditional narrative mode" to bear on his battered life with Lydia Ketterer: "I did not know such depths of humiliation were possible. . . ." Moreover, Zuckerman, and later Tarnopol, will insist that even the once-valued parallels to art no longer apply:

A reader of Conrad's *Lord Jim* and Mauriac's *Thérèse* and Kafka's "Letter to His Father," of Hawthorne and Strindberg and Sophocles—of Freud!—and still I did not know that humiliation could do such a job on a

114

man. . . . For I cannot fully believe in the hopelessness of
my predicament, and yet the line that concludes *The
Trial* is as familiar to me as my own face: "it was
as if the shame of it must outlive him"! Only I am
not a character in a book, certainly not *that* book. I am
real. And my humiliation is equally *real*. (86)

The Zuckerman stories are, indeed, "Useful Fictions," ones that provide a warm up for the main bout
between Peter Tarnopol and Lydia's "real-life" counterpart, Maureen Johnson Tarnopol. More than any
other contemporary writer, with the possible exception
of Norman Mailer, Philip Roth has been relentless
about probing the connections between his private pas-
sions (kvetches, griefs, failures) and the larger mythologies that make up contemporary American life. Marriage is a rich subject for such analysis, although *My
Life as a Man* is hardly the book one would write if he
could choose otherwise. Tarnopol's saga—entitled, significantly enough, "My True Story"—is an effort to
climb out of bottomless pain, to "have it out," to know,
at last, what the truth of his marriage really was. In this
sense, *My Life as a Man* reminds us of Hemingway's
"The Snows of Kilimanjaro" or Fitzgerald's "The
Crack-Up." Nothing quite succeeds in American let-
ters like failure, especially when a youthful talent lies
perpetually unfulfilled. Granted, Tarnopol, unlike the
swaggering crew who preceded him in American literature is not brought low by booze and/or big parties.
His albatross, being the casualty of a marital failure,
is more commonplace, but the effects at the writing
desk are much the same.

Roth's own driving compulsions are, at best, only
thinly disguised in the robes of Tarnopol. His invective about divorce is simultaneously brave and foolish:
brave, because Tarnopol's marriage is laid so bare that

it takes on a collective importance; foolish, because novels cannot run on strident energy alone. Roth manages a delicate equipoise between the *illusion* of helter-skelter confession–rationalization and the artistic "fact" of Tarnopol's more cohesive identity.

At times Tarnopol adopts the coolly rational tone one associates with an Op-Ed column from the *New York Times* (where, in fact, the following section of *My Life as a Man* first appeared):

> The extent of the panic and rage aroused by the issue of alimony, the ferocity displayed by people who were otherwise sane and civilized enough, testifies, I think, to the shocking—and humiliating—realization that came to couples in the courtroom about the fundamental role each may actually have played in the other's life. "So it has descended to this," the enraged contestants might say, glaring in hatred at one another—but even that was only an attempt to continue to hide from the most humiliating fact of all: that it really was this, all along. (117)

More characteristic, however, is the bald outrage Tarnopol feels when he remembers how Maureen tricked him into such an unmanning marriage:

> It is not that easy for me to tell it today [that Maureen had rigged her pregnancy test] without at least a touch of vertigo. And I have never been able to introduce the story into a work of fiction, not that I haven't repeatedly tried and failed in the five years since I received Maureen's confession. I cannot seem to make it credible—probably because I still don't entirely believe it myself. How could she? To me! No matter how I may contrive to transform low actuality into high art, that is invariably what is emblazoned across the face of the narrative, in blood: HOW COULD SHE? TO ME? (208)

Earlier, I suggested in passing that *My Life as a Man* might be regarded as a kind of failed *Ulysses*.

It is now time to amplify some of the implications of that statement. Joyce's novel is not only *about* domestic life, it is a celebration (albeit, a qualified, ironically cast one) of that condition. Conjugal life with Nora changed Joyce; rather than squandering his manhood (Tarnopol's complaint), he discovered it in ways that have nothing to do with *machismo* and everything to do with a comprehensive vision of the world. With *Ulysses*, Joyce splits himself into the eternal son we know as Stephen Dedalus and the comic Jewish father we call Leopold Bloom. June 16, 1904, is a day crowded with events and data, but, for Bloom, no moment looms larger than Molly's impending cuckoldry with Blazes Boylan. Painful memories of the past—the suicide of his father/the death of his infant son—dovetail into his present situation as a guilt-ridden husband about to be unmanned.

Much of the novel militates against Bloom's achieving heroic stature; if he is a mythic counterpart of Ulysses, it is a Ulysses in very small proportions indeed. At the same time, however, he may well be the only hero possible in a Modernist age. In his boundless enthusiasms, his indefatigable curiosity and, most of all, in his compassion, Bloom teaches Stephen those truths of the heart conspicuously absent in all the airy talk about aesthetic theory. To imagine, as Stephen does, that art can occur only after one has flown past the nets of family, Church, and State is to forget that these are the very subjects worth writing about. Indeed, they are all one can write about.

Joyce, of course, knew full well that the history of Stephen's "liberation" in *A Portrait of the Artist of a Young Man* and its anguishing consequences in *Ulysses* were worth the telling, but he also knew that Bloom's bumbling responses to a troubled marriage could tell us even more of what it is to be fully human. Bloom, of course, will never write a *Ulysses*, however much he might dream about placing a story in *Tit Bits*, payment at the rate of one guinea a column. But neither will the grimly serious Mr. Dedalus. Only a blending of the two temperaments could manage that!

What I am pointing toward, of course, is Joyce's sense of aesthetic distance and artistic maturity, commodities largely missing in the agonized landscape of *My Life as a Man*. Rather than the "God of the creation, who remains within or behind or beyond or above his handiwork, invisible, refined out of existence, indifferent, paring his fingernails," Roth's protagonist rages against the dimming of his artistic light (via Maureen) and the injustice that tricked him into marriage. If *he* had believed in the "responsibilities" due a woman you have impregnated, how could *she* euchre him with faked urine?

The most memorable scenes in *My Life as a Man* are those played closest to the bone: the bra-and-panties he "wears" as symbols of his self-abasement, battling divorce lawyers (à la Norman Mailer), fantasizing a Hoffritz hunting knife and bloody revenges, the "lecture" at Brooklyn College he cannot deliver. Not since Karl Shapiro's saddening novel *Edsel* has an established writer been so insistent about the tenuous connections between failed talent and "sensitivity." Reduced as both a man *and* a once-promising writer, Tarnopol can only squeeze the iron pillar of a subway platform and try desperately to *"Hang on!"* Peter Tarnopol, author of *A Jewish Father* (1959), cannot be a "man," much less a *father*, himself!

At the same time, however, the novel's substructure of literary comparisons—Tarnopol's life is, presumably, more hellish than *The Trial*, more compulsive than "A Death in Venice,"—works on that principle of contradiction that makes a work like Keats's "Ode on a Nightingale" a great poem about the purity of song no *poem* can ever match. That is, *failure* operates as both the subject and the mode by which Keats's work of art achieves its stunning success.

In this sense too, Tarnopol's ill-fated interludes with Karen Oakes (the willing student all "with-it" writers fantasize about) and Susan Seabury McCall (who offers much the same brand of gourmet cooking and uncomplicated aid and comfort as Ramona extended to Moses Herzog) reenforce the depth of "failure" in *My Life as a Man*. As Maureen suggests in her journal: "I could be his Muse, if only he'd let me." Significantly enough, the remark provides Tarnopol with an epigraph for his novel and Roth with a "ghost" more haunting than Gothic writers could imagine. Tarnopol puts it this way:

> I would have laughed had anyone suggested that struggling with a woman over a marriage would come to occupy me in the way that exploring the South Pole had occupied Admiral Byrd—or writing *Madame Bovary* had occupied Flaubert. Clearly the last thing I could have imagined myself, a dissident and skeptical member of my generation, succumbing to all that moralizing rhetoric about "permanent relationships." And, in truth, it did take something more than the rhetoric to do me in. It took Maureen, wielding it. (173)

And in Tarnopol *Roth* finds that voice he can sustain even more convincingly than he could through Portnoy. Dr. Spielvogel (given lines he was systematically denied in *Portnoy's Complaint*) writes Tarnopol down in a single word, *narcissistic*. The term might well apply to all of Roth's protagonists, but it is Tarnopol whom Roth strips with a lacerating energy unparalleled in his earlier work. To be sure, Maureen gets the sort of lumps one expects from a misogynist like Roth, but, this time, the confessional impulse distributes "blame" more evenly: This time his castrated male can admit that "I was fooled by appearances, largely my own."

Finally, a word or two about the disturbing implications of a title like *My Life as a Man*: Talk about "manhood" strikes me, more often than not, as running a gamut from the boring to the downright embarrassing. Chalk it up to "candor" or what you will, but I would prefer not being pulled into the fray. Unfortunately, Roth's title makes that impossible. Let me suggest, therefore, that, like the French lieutenant in Conrad's *Lord Jim* who was asked about cowardice, Roth "knows nothing of it." By this I mean to imply two things: (1) That Roth's *My Life as a Man* is, indeed, a courageous book, one that spells out the horrors of a failed marriage in ruthless detail and (2) that it is also a book which makes it painfully clear Roth is on surer ground when providing a geography of what manhood is not than he is when speculating about what it might be.

Because Philip Roth has built a precedent of changing gears with each new novel, of refusing to build his next book on the foundations of his last one, critical predictions about him are made at one's peril. A few years ago, for example, I was *convinced* that *The Breast* constituted the first volume of a projected trilogy; I even had a good idea about what the other two titles might be. Luckily, I did not make the announcement publicly, although Roth may make a prophet of me yet.

This much at least is clear: Peter Tarnopol ends

My Life as a Man in hibernation at the Quaysay writers' colony, licking his wounds and/or shoring up his
fragments against his ruins. I presume the pun on
"Quaysay" is very much intended. Philip Roth, on the
other hand, continues to be a regular visitor at Yaddo,
where (unlike Tarnopol) he is that colony's most dis-
ciplined and productive writer. Roth's next book, we
are told, will be a collection of essays "imagining" *other*
writers, many of which have already appeared in
places like *The New York Review of Books* and the
New American Review. But it is Roth's own fiction
which a growing number of readers wait for. He has
taught us all how painfully complicated it is to laugh.
Nothing may be more important where surviving the
seventies is concerned. Which is to say, Roth's next
lessons are likely to be even more crucial than his last
ones were.